Fishamble: The New Play Company and Staatstheater
Mainz, in association with Pavilion Theatre
and Lime Tree Theatre | Belltable, present

REFUGE

by Deirdre Kinahan

Refuge was first performed at Staatstheater Mainz, Germany,
on 18 June 2026.

REFUGE
by Deirdre Kinahan

Cast

Hannah	Hannah von Peinen
Molly	Mary Murray
Zabi	Sabah Qalo
Herr Ireland	Aidan Kelly
Peter	Holger Kraft
Musician	Steve Wickham
Dancer	Matthew Williamson

Creative Team

Director	Jim Culleton
Set Designer	Matthias Werner
Costume Designer	Lina Maria Stein
Lighting Designer	Ulrich Schneider
Composer	Steve Wickham
Sound Designer	Axel Heintzenberg
Choreographer	Matthew Williamson
Dramaturg (Ireland)	Gavin Kostick
Dramaturg (Germany)	Boris C. Motzki
Assistant Director	Dalilah Hamam
Literary Assistant (Ireland)	Róisín Daly
Irish translation	Bríd Ní Neachtain
Pashto translation	Zabi Ullah Ahmad Zai

Production Team

Producer (Ireland)	Laura MacNaughton
Artistic Production/ Dramaturg (Germany)	Jörg Vorhaben
Artistic Production (Germany)	Katharina Greuel
Production Manager (Ireland)	Eoin Kilkenny
Production Manager (Germany)	Niels Sonnemann
Stage Manager (Ireland)	Emily Waters
Stage Manager (Germany)	Lisa Passow
Prompter/Surtitles (Germany)	Susanne Pohl
Relighter (Ireland)	Archer Bradshaw
Assistant Producer (Ireland)	Evie McGuinness
Marketing (Ireland)	Allie Whelan
PR (Ireland)	O'Doherty Communications
General Manager (Ireland)	Sarah Bragg-Bolger
Executive Director (Ireland)	Eva Scanlan

The production runs for approximately 80 minutes, with no interval.

Refuge was co-produced by Fishamble and Staatstheater Mainz, opening in Mainz in June 2026, then running in Pavilion Theatre as part of Dublin Theatre Festival and Lime Tree Theatre in Limerick, before returning to Berlin and Mainz for a second run during Ireland's Presidency of the EU. The production was supported by the Arts Council, Dublin City Council, Culture Ireland, the Embassy of Ireland in Germany, the Irish Consulate in Frankfurt and Goethe-Institut.

Special thanks to Margaret O'Riada and Nora Corcoran at the Galway Traveller Movement, the Irish Palatine Heritage Centre in Rathkeale, Don Bosco Care, the Afghan Community and Cultural Association of Ireland, and Zabi Ullah Ahmad Zai, for their help and advice throughout the development of this play.

Acknowledgements

Thanks to the following for their help with this production: Liz Meaney, Bea Kelleher, Maeve Giles, Ciara Coyne, Jesse Weaver, and all at the Arts Council; Ray Yeates, Sinéad Connolly, and all at Dublin City Council Arts Office; Sharon Barry, Ciarán Walsh, and all at Culture Ireland; Eugene Downes and all at the Department of Foreign Affairs; Ambassador Maeve Collins, Candice Gordon, and all at the Embassy of Ireland in Germany; Anne-Marie Flynn and all at the Consulate General of Ireland in Frankfurt; Noémie Njangiru, Heidrun Rottke and all at the Goethe-Institut Ireland; Matt Applewhite, Beth Archer and Maddie Hindes at Nick Hern Books; Belvedere College; all at 3 Great Denmark Street; Róise Goan, Dee Patton, and all at Dublin Theatre Festival; Ronan Fingleton, Dónal Kennedy, Leda Connaughton-Deeny, Ping Ní Chléirigh-Ng, and all at Pavilion; Louise Donlon and all at Lime Tree Theatre; Oein de Bhairduin; all those who have helped since this publication went to print.

About Fishamble

Fishamble is an Irish theatre company that discovers, develops and produces new plays of national importance with a global reach. It has toured its productions to audiences throughout Ireland, and to 22 other countries. It champions the role of the playwright, typically supporting over 50% of the writers of all new plays produced on the island of Ireland each year. It has a number of award-winning outreach and education initiatives which it runs with partners in Dublin and elsewhere. Fishamble has received many awards in Ireland and internationally, including an Olivier Award.

'excellent Fishamble…Ireland's terrific Fishamble' **The Guardian**

'Ireland's leading new writing company' **The Stage**

'the much-loved Fishamble [is] a global brand with international theatrical presence…an unswerving force for new writing' **The Irish Times**

'the respected Dublin company…forward-thinking Fishamble' **The New York Times**

'when Fishamble is [in New York], you've got to go' **Time Out New York**

'that great Irish new writing company, Fishamble' **Lyn Gardner, Stage Door**

'the superb Irish company Fishamble' **The Scotsman**

'Fishamble puts electricity into the National grid of dreams' **Sebastian Barry**

Fishamble Staff: Jim Culleton (Artistic Director & CEO), Eva Scanlan (Executive Director), Gavin Kostick (Literary Manager), Laura MacNaughton (Producer), Sarah Bragg-Bolger (General Manager), Allie Whelan (Marketing, Outreach, and Engagement Manager), Evie McGuinness (Assistant Producer), Róisín Daly (Literary Assistant)

Fishamble Board: John McGrane, Ronan Nulty, John O'Donnell, Siobhan O'Leary (Chair), Colleen Savage, Christine Sisk, John Tierney, Denise Walshe (Vice Chair)

Former Chairs of Fishamble: Eoin Kennelly, Andrew Parkes (Honorary Life Member), Doireann Ní Bhriain

Fishamble is funded by the Arts Council, Dublin City Council, and Culture Ireland.

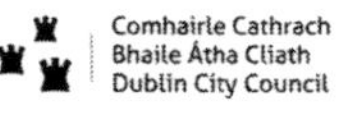

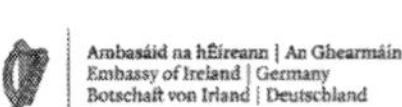

Fishamble Productions

First time and early career playwrights

Fishamble has produced many plays by first time playwrights, including *Don Juan* by Michael West in 1990, *Howling Moons, Silent Sons* by Deirdre Hines in 1991, *The Ash Fire* by Gavin Kostick in 1992, *Red Roses and Petrol* by Joseph O'Connor in 1994, *From Both Hips* by Mark O'Rowe in 1997, *The Nun's Wood* by Pat Kinevane in 1998, and *Noah And The Tower Flower* by Sean McLoughlin (Irish Times Best New Play Award winner) in 2007. Many of these plays won the Stewart Parker Trust Award for new playwrights. Recent plays by new and emerging writers include:

- *The Black Wolfe Tone* by Kwaku Fortune (2025), touring in Ireland and New York, in co-production with the Irish Repertory Theatre
- *In Two Minds* by Joanne Ryan (2023–25) touring in Ireland, UK, and US
- *Breaking* by Amy Kidd (2024) in Dublin Theatre Festival and on tour
- *Duck Duck Goose* by Caitríona Daly (2021–22) touring in Ireland, and online
- *The Humours of Bandon* by Margaret McAuliffe (since 2017) touring in Ireland, UK, US, and Australia
- *Charolais* by Noni Stapleton (2017) in New York
- *Swing* by Steve Blount, Peter Daly, Gavin Kostick and Janet Moran (2014–16) touring in Ireland, UK, Europe, US, Australia and New Zealand
- *The Wheelchair on My Face* by Sonya Kelly (2013–14) touring in Ireland, UK, Europe and US, winner of Scotsman Fringe First award.

Established playwrights

Fishamble has ongoing relationships with many of Ireland's top playwrights. Recent productions include:

- *Refuge* by Deirdre Kinahan (2026) in co-production with Staatstheater Mainz, in association with Pavilion and Lime Tree Theatre | Belltable, in Dublin Theatre Festival, Limerick and Germany
- *For Dolores* by Eva O'Connor (2026) in association with Lime Tree Theatre | Belltable, Galway International Arts Festival, and Traverse Theatre
- *The Leap* by Gavin Kostick (2025) in Dublin Theatre Festival and touring to DEIS schools in Dublin's North East Inner City
- *Heaven* by Eugene O'Brien (2022–25) touring in Ireland, UK, and US, winner of Scotsman Fringe First, Irish Times Best Play and Irish Times Best Actress (for Janet Moran) awards
- *Mustard* by Eva O'Connor (2020–24) on tour in Ireland, internationally, and online, in co-production with Sunday's Child, winner of Scotsman Fringe First Award
- *The Pride of Parnell Street* by Sebastian Barry (2007–11, and 2022) touring in Ireland, and internationally, BBC Audio, multi award-winning
- *On Blueberry Hill* by Sebastian Barry (2017–21) touring in Ireland, Europe, Off-Broadway, West End, Audible, and online

- *Rathmines Road* by Deirdre Kinahan (2018) in coproduction with the Abbey Theatre
- *Mainstream* by Rosaleen McDonagh (2016) in coproduction with Project Arts Centre
- *Little Thing, Big Thing* by Donal O'Kelly (2014–16) touring in Ireland, UK, Europe, US and Australia, winner of The Stage Award.

Pat Kinevane

Fishamble is very proud of its long-term relationship with Pat Kinevane whose solo plays it has commissioned, developed, produced and toured since 2006. These are *Forgotten* (since 2006), *Silent* (since 2011), *Underneath* (since 2014), *Before* (since 2018) and *King* (since 2023). These productions have toured in Ireland, UK, Europe, US, Australia, New Zealand, India, and online, in English, and bilingually in many countries. Fishamble and Pat Kinevane have won Olivier, Herald Angel, Stage Raw, Scotsman Fringe First, Herald Archangel, Argus Angel, Origin Best Production, and Helen Hayes awards.

International play development partnerships

Fishamble often partners with other arts organisations to develop new work, often by artists that have been underrepresented in Irish theatre. For instance, *Turning Point* in 2010 was a festival of work by Irish writers with disabilities in partnership with ADI and VSA, which toured to the Kennedy Center in Washington, D.C. Recent initiatives include:

- *Not Beckett* by Jennifer Barclay, Felispeaks, Olwen Fouéré, Hannah Khalil, and Nicola McCartney (2024–25), in partnership with Irish Repertory Theatre, Villanova, Reading University, Citizens Theatre
- *Transatlantic Commissions Residency* by Felispeaks, Kwaku Fortune, Jade Jordan, and CN Smith (2024) in Dublin and New York, in partnership with the Irish Repertory Theatre and in association with the Apollo
- *Murdered Men Do Drip and Bleed* by Hannah Khalil and Jennifer Barclay (2023), in Dublin and online, in partnership with Washington, D.C. companies Mosaic and Solas Nua
- *On the Horizon* by Shannon Yee, Hefin Robinson, Michael Patrick, Oisín Kearney, Samantha O'Rourke, Ciara Elizabeth Smyth, Connor Allen (2021) online, in association with Dirty Protest.

Political plays

Fishamble has produced many plays that help us grapple with the world in which we live, sometimes focusing on historical events as part of the government's *Decade of Centenaries* programme. Many of these productions are site-specific or happen off-site. These include:

- *The Navigator Project*–short plays about healthcare inequality by Susannah Al Fraihat, Carys D. Coburn, Ryan Gillespie, Jade Jordan, Hannah Khalil, Susan Lynch, Caitlin Magnall-Kearns, Rosaleen McDonagh, Niall Murphy, and Treasa Nealon (2026)
- *"Certain Individual Women"* by Julie Morrissy (2024) on national tour

- *Outrage* by Deirdre Kinahan (2022 and 2024) touring and online, in association with Dublin Port Company and Meath County Council

- *The Treaty* by Colin Murphy (2021–22) in Ireland, Irish Embassy in London, and online as part of the Seóda Festival

- *Embargo* by Deirdre Kinahan (2020) online, during Dublin Theatre Festival, in association with Dublin Port Company and Irish Rail

- *The Alternative* by Oisín Kearney and Michael Patrick (2019) in association with Pavilion Theatre, Draíocht, Belltable, Everyman Theatre, Town Hall Theatre, and Lyric Theatre, winner of Irish Times Best Sound Design (for Denis Clohessy) and Best Director (for Jim Culleton) awards

- *Haughey | Gregory* by Colin Murphy (2018–19) in the Abbey Theatre, Mountjoy Prison, Dáil Éireann, Croke Park, and Larkin Community College, as well as on national tour

- *Maz & Bricks* by Eva O'Connor (2017–18) in Ireland, UK and US

- *GPO 1818* by Colin Murphy (2018) staged in the GPO to mark its bicentenary

- *Inside the GPO* by Colin Murphy (2016) performed in the GPO on the centenary of the Easter Rising, and screened internationally online

- *Tiny Plays for Ireland and America* by 26 writers (2016) at the Kennedy Center, Washington, D.C., and Irish Arts Center, New York, as part of *Ireland 100*

- *Bailed Out* (2015) and *Guaranteed* (2013) by Colin Murphy, on national tour.

International touring

Many of Fishamble's productions have toured internationally, in partnership with a network of festivals and venues, including: Soho Theatre, Trafalgar Theatre, Southwark Playhouse, Kiln, Arcola in London; Traverse, Summerhall, Assembly in Edinburgh; 59E59 Theaters, Origin, Irish Arts Center, Irish Repertory Theatre in New York; Odyssey in Los Angeles; Solas Nua in Washington, D.C.; Kolkata Centre for Creativity, Rajasthan International Centre in India; APA, Merrigong, Vessel in Australia. Recent international tours include:

- *The Black Wolfe Tone* by Kwaku Fortune (2025), touring in Ireland and New York, in co-production with the Irish Repertory Theatre

- *In Two Minds* by Joanne Ryan (2023–25) touring in Ireland, UK, and US

- *Heaven* by Eugene O'Brien (2022–25) touring in Ireland, UK, and US, winner of the Scotsman Fringe First, Irish Times Best Play and Irish Times Best Actress (for Janet Moran) awards

- *Fight Night* by Gavin Kostick (2025) in New York, in association with Rise Productions

- *Taigh/Tŷ/Teach* by Eva O'Connor, Màiri Morrison, and Mared Llywelyn Williams (2024–25) in Kerry, touring to Scotland and Wales, online and in cinemas, in partnership with Theatre Gu Leòr and Theatr Bara Caws

- *On Blueberry Hill* by Sebastian Barry (2017–21) touring in Ireland, Europe, Off-Broadway, West End, Audible, and online

- *Mustard* by Eva O'Connor (since 2020) on tour in Ireland, internationally, and online

- *The Humours of Bandon* by Margaret McAuliffe (since 2017) touring in Ireland, UK, US, and Australia
- *Drip Feed* by Karen Cogan (2018) in coproduction with Soho Theatre, touring in Ireland and UK
- *Little Thing, Big Thing* by Donal O'Kelly (2014–16) touring in Ireland, UK, Europe, US and Australia
- *Swing* by Steve Blount, Peter Daly, Gavin Kostick and Janet Moran (2014–16) touring in Ireland, UK, Europe, US, Australia and New Zealand.

Other artforms and media

Fishamble often shares filmed versions of its plays online, in cinemas, and through its *Encore* programme in schools. It produced a series of radio plays for RTÉ lyric fm, and has also recorded audio versions of its productions for Audible, BBC, and RTÉ Radio One. It has worked across disciplines, including *Invitation to a Journey* by David Bolger, Deirdre Gribbin and Gavin Kostick (2016) in coproduction with CoisCeim, Crash Ensemble and Galway International Arts Festival. It produced two seasons of tiny plays online: .

- *Tiny Plays for a Brighter Future* by Niall Murphy, Signe Lury, Eva-Jane Gaffney (2021) online, in association with ESB
- *Tiny Plays 24/7* by Lora Hartin, Maria Popovic, Ciara Elizabeth Smyth, Caitríona Daly, Conor Hanratty, Julia Marks, Patrick O'Laoghaire, Eric O'Brien, Grace Lobo, Ryan Murphy (2020) online.

Fishamble wishes to thank the following Friends of Fishamble & Corporate Members for their invaluable support:

ATM Accounting Services, Doireann Ní Bhriain, Dearbhail & Michael Bermingham, Colette and Barry Breen, Sean Brett, John Butler, Ann-Marie Carroll, Betsy Carroll, Breda Cashe, Finola & Michael Earley, Stewart Harrington, Andrew Hetherington, Geoffrey & Jane Keating, Lisney, Liz Kelly, Stephen & Susan Lambert, Damian Lane, Angus Laverty, Pat McIntyre, Ger McNaughton, Anne McQuillan, Regina McQuillan, Louise Molloy, Anne Moloney, David Nelson, James Nugent, Ronan Nulty, Tom O'Connor, Siobhan O'Leary, Andrew & Delyth Parkes, Kevin Rafter, Judy Regan, Royal County Furniture, Eileen Ryan, Colleen Savage, Derry Scanlan, Brian Singleton, Eddie Soye, Mary Stephenson, Patrick Vassel and Denise Walshe.

fishamble.com   facebook.com/fishamble   twitter.com/fishamble

Biographies

'**Deirdre Kinahan** is one of Ireland's major contemporary playwrights. She writes about issues that affect modern Ireland as well as the issues that have clouded its past. She is a masterful, poetic writer, with a way with a phrase that just dazzles.' (*The Slotkin Letter, Canada, Review*)

An award-winning playwright, Deirdre is a member of Aosdána, Ireland's elected affiliation of outstanding artists. She collaborates with artists and theatres all over the world, is literary associate to Meath County Council and has a large canon of regularly produced plays to her credit. Deirdre's plays have been translated into many languages. She is published by Nick Hern Books.

Recent works include *The Saviour* (Landmark Productions & Irish Repertory Theatre New York, 2023), *An Old Song Half Forgotten* (Abbey Theatre & Sofft Productions, 2023), *TEMPESTA* (Glass Mask Theatre/Cork Midsummer Festival, 2024), *Bloody Yesterday* (Glass Mask Theatre, 2022), *In the Middle of the Fields* (Solas Nua, Washington DC, 2021), *The Visit* (Draíocht & Dublin Theatre Festival, 2021/22), *Rathmines Road* (Abbey Theatre & Fishamble, 2018) and her Irish Revolutionary Trilogy, written as part of the national commemorations, *OUTRAGE/EMBARGO/ WILD SKY*.

Deirdre has a number of new theatre projects premiering in 2026; *REFUGE* for Staatstheater Mainz in Germany & Fishamble in Ireland, *ADRIFT* for NOMAD Touring Network, *The Homecoming of Joseph Grace* for Cork Midsummer Festival & Pavilion Theatre, *EXILE* for Meath County Council & Dublin Port. She is also under commission to Landmark Productions, An Taibhdhearc and Fishamble. She has years of experience as a producer and enjoys curating or participating in multi-genre artistic projects for Meath County Council and other national festivals/events.

Representation: Emily Hickman at The Agency London.

Jim Culleton is the artistic director of Fishamble: The New Play Company, for which he has directed productions on tour throughout Ireland, UK, Europe, Australia, India, New Zealand, Canada and the US, including 11 transfers off-Broadway. His productions for Fishamble have won Olivier, The Stage, Scotsman Fringe First, and Irish Times Best Director awards.

Jim has directed for the Abbey, the Gaiety, the Belgrade, Staatstheater Mainz, 7:84 Scotland, Project, Amharclann de híde, Tinderbox, Passion Machine, the Ark, Second Age, Dundee Rep, CoisCéim/Crash Ensemble/GIAF, Little Museum of Dublin, Fighting Words, Scripts, Dirty Protest, Draíocht, and Baptiste Programme. He has directed audio plays for Audible, BBC, RTÉ Radio 1, and RTÉ lyric fm.

He has also directed for Vessel and APA (Australia), Solas Nua, Mosaic, and Kennedy Center (Washington DC), Odyssey (LA), Origin, Irish Arts Center, New Dramatists, Irish Rep, and 59E59 (New York), as well as for Trafalgar Theatre Productions on the West End, and IAC/Symphony Space on Broadway.

Jim has taught for NYU, NUI, GSA, Uversity, the Lir, Villanova, Notre Dame, UM, UMD, JNU, TU Dublin, Drexel, and TCD. He has edited many books, most recently *Fishamble Tiny Plays* for New Island Books.

Hannah von Peinen studied acting at HMTM Hannover. During this time, she performed at the Schauspielhaus Hamburg and the Staatstheater Hannover and received a solo award at the 2000 drama school meeting. After a year at the Grips Theater Berlin, she joined the national theatre of Mannheim from 2002–08, where she appeared as Medea, Desdemona, Hermia, Klärchen, and Amalia, among others. She worked with many different directors, for example: Cilli Drexel, KD Schmidt, Sebastian Baumgarten, Thomas Langhoff, Niklas Helbling, Burkhard C. Kosminski, and Simon Solberg.

After a two-year stay in Los Angeles, she joined Theater Bielefeld from 2010 to 2012, where she worked with Christian Schlüter, Cilli Drexel, Daniela Kranz, and Dariusch Yazdkhasti, among others. From 2012 to 2018, she worked as a freelancer and made several guest appearances at the Nationaltheater Mannheim, including as Nora H. Ibsen directed by Cilli Drexel, the Theater Bielefeld, Theater Freiburg, Vagantenbühne Berlin, and Ballhaus Ost. During this time, she worked with Sebastian Schug, Bettina Rehm, Christian Schlüter, and repeatedly with the Prinzip Gonzo collective.

Since 2018, she has been a member of the ensemble at the Mainz State Theater and has appeared as Queen Elizabeth in *Maria Stuart*, directed by Dariusch Yazdkhasti, Myrtle Gordon in *Opening Night*, directed by Wolfgang Menardi, Olga in *Three Sisters*, directed by Maren E. Bjorseth, Clytemnestra *Electra* directed by Alexander Nerlich, and Sandra in Deirdre Kinahan's *Rathmines Road*, directed by Kathrin Mädler, among others.

Hannah von Peinen lives with her family in Mainz and Berlin

hannahvonpeinen.de

Mary Murray's stage performances have toured Europe, China and the United States. She received Best Actress and Best Supporting Actress awards with MAMCA, The First Irish Theatre Festival in New York and The Irish Times. Her favourite roles to date include: Bessie Burgess in *The Plough and the Stars* (Abbey Theatre), *Cosima* – a one woman show, *Holy Mary* (Breda Cashe Productions), Janet in *The Pride of Parnell Street*, Nell in *Outrage*, and Natalie in *Noah and the Tower Flower* (Fishamble: The New Play Company), *No Smoke Without Fire* – a one woman show (Viking Theatre), *Ulysses* (Tron Theatre) *On Raftery's Hill* (Druid/Royal Court).

She has over 60 screen credits. She was nominated for Best Actress and Best Supporting Actress at the Irish Film and Television Awards for her role as Janet in *Love/Hate*. Other notable productions include *Valhalla, Penny Dreadful, Adam and Paul, The Magdalene Sisters, Dead Still* and *Let the Wrong One In*.

She voiced numerous animations and radio plays and she's the recipient of the Best Actress Award at the BBC Audio Drama Awards for her performance in *The Pride of Parnell Street*, produced by Fishamble: The New Play Company.

Mary is the director of Visions Drama School www.visionsdrama.com

You can find out more about her on her website www.marymurrayirishactress.com

Sabah Qalo was born in Kirkuk, Iraq, in 1995. He came to Germany in 2009, attended high school in Vreden until graduating with his intermediate school leaving certificate, and trained as a hotel manager in Augsburg. At the same time, he spent a year acting with the Junges Team Theater Augsburg and then three years with the theater ensemble e.V.

In 2022, he completed his acting studies at the Frankfurt University of Music and Performing Arts.

In 2021, he received the Germany Scholarship from the HfMDK Frankfurt.

Sabah Qalo has been a member of the acting ensemble at the Mainz State Theater since 2022. In 2025, he brought his solo evening *Hakawati – eine Reise* (*Hakawati – A Journey*) to the stage.

Aidan Kelly's previous work for Fishamble: *Inside the GPO, The Pride of Parnell Street*.

Theatre includes: *Poor, A View from the Bridge* (Gate theatre, Dublin); *Fear of 13, The Man Who Had All The Luck* (Donmar Warehouse); *Salome, Treasure Island, The Silver Tassie* (National Theatre, London); *Macbeth, Troilus and Cressida, The Merchant of Venice* (RSC); *Once the Musical* (West End); *Last Orders at the Dockside, The Country Girls, Macbeth, True West, Howie the Rookie, Doubt, The

Plough and the Stars, Juno and the Paycock, The Resistible Rise of Arturo Ui, The Barbaric Comedies, The Burial at Thebes, Sucking Dublin (Abbey Theatre); *The Misfits* (Corn Exchange); *Long Day's Journey into Night, The Playboy of The Western World, The Good Father, Philadelphia, Here I Come!* (Druid Theatre).

TV/Film includes: *Say Nothing* (Disney), *Stay Close* (Netflix), *Warrior* (HBO), *Killing Eve, Call the Midwife, Fair City*.

Holger Kraft was born in Rüsselsheim in 1971 and grew up there. After studying acting at the University of Music and Theater in Leipzig, his first permanent engagement was at the Theaterhaus in Jena, where he enjoyed four successful years under the direction of Claudia Bauer. This was followed by engagements as a freelance actor in Berlin, Freiburg, Stuttgart, and Erlangen before he joined the Wuppertaler Bühnen in 2009.

In 2012, Kraft left his engagement in Wuppertal to return to freelance acting, including as a lecturer in acting at the Academy of Performing Arts in Ludwigsburg.

In 2016, Holger Kraft then moved to Theater Bonn, where he worked until recently. Holger Kraft is co-founder of Theaterhaus Sechzig90 Rüsselsheim, which has made a name for itself as an artistic community of interest.

Steve Wickham studied violin at the Royal College of Music, Dublin, and has developed a distinctive career as a composer and performer across theatre, film, and contemporary music. He has collaborated extensively with The Abbey Theatre, contributing music and performance to productions by Michael Harding and Tom MacIntyre, including *Caoineadh Airt Uí Laoghaire* and *Cúirt an Mheán Oíche*, as well as *Sleeping a Lovesong* and *Bogdances*. His theatre work combines live performance with immersive soundscape, often placing music at the dramatic centre of the stage action. In 2023, he was nominated for an Irish Times Theatre Awards award for Best Soundscape for Carpet Theatre's *Breath*, in which he also performed. He has composed and acted in plays by Deirdre Kinahan, including *Tempesta* and *Refuge*, and in *The Hare* by Bob Kelly and Clare Monnelly, touring nationally in 2023–24.

Beyond theatre, Wickham is widely recognised for his long-standing role with *The Waterboys* and for collaborations with artists including U2 and Sinéad O'Connor. He has also released eight albums with his own band, *NoCrows*, and composed original scores for film.

Based in the northwest of Ireland, he continues to create work in which music and drama intersect, both on stage and screen.

Matthew Williamson is an award-winning Dancer and Movement Director whose work has been presented nationally and internationally across theatre, dance and large-scale spectacle. Known for a rigorous physical language and a refined dramaturgical sensibility, his practice is rooted in collaboration and driven by a deep engagement with text, space and ensemble.

His extensive body of work includes *The Dead, Hammam, Lolling, An Truen, Staging the Treaty, The Lost O'Casey, The Book Of Names, These Rooms, Faultline* and *The Anvil*, among many others. Across these productions, he has developed a reputation for crafting movement that is both architecturally precise and emotionally resonant, enhancing narrative through meticulous physical detail and dynamic spatial composition.

He has collaborated with leading companies including Anu Productions, Landmark Productions, CoisCéim Dance Theatre and Macnas, contributing to work that spans intimate site-responsive performance to epic, large-scale theatrical events. His work has been presented at major international and national venues and festivals including the Sydney Opera House, MIF and the Abbey Theatre, reflecting both the scale and ambition of his artistic reach.

Central to his approach is a commitment to ensemble-driven process and the cultivation of bold, embodied storytelling. Whether reimagining canonical texts or developing new work, he brings a distinctive clarity and sophistication to each project, shaping performances that are visually compelling and theatrically rigorous.

Through an ongoing exploration of movement as narrative Matthew continues to contribute significantly to contemporary performance practice, creating work that is formally inventive, intellectually grounded and viscerally immediate.

Matthias Werner, born in Nordhausen, trained as an interior designer before studying architecture at the Bauhaus Weimar. From 2000 to 2006, he worked as a stage design assistant with Jan Pappelbaum at the Schaubühne am Lehniner Platz, the Theater Nordhausen, and the Saarländisches Staatstheater Saarbrücken, among others. Since 2004, he has been designing his own stage sets and costumes at the Schauspiel Stuttgart, Maxim Gorki Theater Berlin, Theater an der Wien/Neue Oper Wien, Schauspielhaus Bochum, Staatstheater Oldenburg, Staatstheater Braunschweig, and Ballhaus Naunynstrasse, among others. He has worked with directors such as Anna Bergmann, Helena Waldmann, Jan Neumann, Hendrik Müller, Neco Celik, Maguerite Donlon, Petra Wüllenweber, and Bob Ziegenbalg. Matthias Werner also designs sets for films, most recently for Ramon Zürcher's *Das merkwürdige Kätzchen* (The Strange Little Cat), which premiered at the 63rd Berlinale in 2013.

Lina Maria Stein, born in 1996 in the Vulkaneifel region, completed her voluntary social year in theater education at the Landestheater Detmold.

While still studying theatre studies at JGU Mainz, she was hired as a set design assistant at the Staatstheater Mainz in 2019 and successfully completed her studies in January 2020. After numerous assistantships in stage and costume design and further training in fashion design and costume history, she went on to create her own sets, collaborate on productions, and design costumes for theater and opera, working with K.D. Schmidt, Mark Reisig, Simone Glatt, Gianluca Falaschi, and Fabio Godinho, among others.

Ulrich Schneider was born in Hamm, Westphalia, in 1962. He studied mining and theatre and event technology in Aachen and Berlin. From 1991 to 1995, he worked at the Schauspielhaus Cologne, most recently as lighting director.

From 1995 to 1999, he worked as lighting director at the Berlin Volksbühne am Rosa-Luxemburg-Platz under artistic director Frank Castorf. From 2001 to 2014, he was lighting designer and lighting director for the Nibelungen Festival in Worms. He held the same position at the Bad Hersfeld Festival from 2015 to 2019. Since January 1, 2020, he has been head of lighting and lighting designer at the Mainz State Theatre.

Since 1999, he has been working as a freelance lighting designer and set designer for opera, musical, theater, and dance productions, as well as in the field of museum and exhibition lighting.

He has worked with directors such as Christoph Marthaler, Lars Ole Walburg, Nikolaus Lehnhoff, Karin Baier, Frank Castorf, Johann Kresnik, Karoline Gruber, Christoph Schlingensief, Vera Nemirowa, and Gil Mehmert for the Vienna State Opera, the Burgtheater Vienna, the Korean National Opera in Seoul, the Schauspielhaus Zurich, Philharmonie Luxembourg, Theater Basel, Kampnagel Hamburg, Staatsoper Stuttgart, Festspielhaus Baden-Baden, Aalto Oper Essen, Opéra de Metz, Schwetzinger Festspiele, Oper Graz, and Bad Hersfelder Festspiele.

In recent years, he has also been responsible for lighting design for world premieres such as *Orlando* by Olga Neu.

Axel Heintzenberg grew up in Babenhausen in southern Hesse and appeared on stage in various musical productions as a teenager. After graduating from high school, he studied music education with a major in singing at Justus Liebig University in Giessen and subsequently worked as a musical director, vocal coach, and choir director.

He was a member of the Darmstadt Concert Choir under the direction of Wolfgang Seeliger, the Petruskantorei in Giessen under the direction of Herfried Mencke, and a founding member of the "Kicks'n'Sticks Voices" (vocal group of the Hesse State Youth Jazz Orchestra) under the direction of Wolfgang Diefenbach. Here he completed numerous work phases and workshops with renowned lecturers (New York Voices, The Real Group, Jeff Cascaro, among others), went on concert tours with the LJJO in China and South Africa, and participated in several CD recordings.

As a sound engineer and music producer, he worked for film and television – including *DEIN SONG* (ZDF/KIKA) and *Das Mädchen und der Flüchtling* (ARD) – and founded his own recording studio in Darmstadt with three colleagues in 2017.

Axel Heintzenberg has been employed at the Mainz State Theater since November 2022. In the 2024/25 season, he can be seen as Charon *in Orpheus. The Art of Losing.*

Outside of the theatre, he continues to work as a vocal coach and composes music for children's musicals.

Gavin Kostick is a playwright, literary manager and independent dramaturg.

His works have been produced nationally and internationally. Favourite works for Fishamble include *The Ash Fire, The Flesh Addict, The End of the Road* and *Invitation to a Journey* (with CoisCéim and Crash Ensemble). *The Leap* is Gavin's first play for children.

Further works include *This is What We Sang for Kabosh, Fight Night, The Games People Play* and *At the Ford* for Rise Productions and *Gym Swim Party* with Danielle Galligan in co-production with the O'Reilly Theatre. He wrote the libretto for the opera *The Alma Fetish* composed by Raymond Deane, performed at the National Concert Hall. As a performer he performed Joseph Conrad's *Heart of Darkness: Complete*, a six hour show for Absolut Fringe, Dublin Theatre Festival and the London Festival of Literature at the Southbank.

Gavin is currently the literary manager of Fishamble: The New Play Company, a tutor in playwriting and dramaturgy in both The Lir Academy and Trinity College Dublin as well as being a core mentor on the Tenderfoot Transition Year programme for young writers at the Civic Theatre.

Particular favourite projects that Gavin has initiated and delivered with Fishamble include Show in a Bag (with Dublin Fringe and The Irish Theatre Institute), The New Play Clinic, The Dublin Fringe New Writing Award, Tiny Plays for Ireland and A Play for Ireland.

Both for Fishamble, and as an independent dramaturg, Gavin's projects and works he has supported have gained significant national and international award recognition including amongst others Irish Times Irish Theatre Awards, BBC Stewart Parker Trust, Zebbie Awards, Dublin Fringe Awards, Business to Arts, Olivier, Scotsman Fringe First, Herald Angel and Archangel and New York Critics' Pick.

His own plays have also received similar national and international award recognition. Gavin has recently completed a new version of *The Odyssey*, supported by Kilkenny Arts Festival, ClassicsNow.

Boris C. Motzki, born in Worms in 1980, studied theatre studies and German philology at Johannes Gutenberg University Mainz (graduating in 2006).

From 2006, he worked as an assistant director at the National Theater Mannheim, where he created his first productions. Since 2009, he has worked as a freelance director, including at the Staatstheater Darmstadt. His productions have been invited to festivals on numerous occasions.

From 2014 to 2017, he was deputy artistic director and head of drama at the Landestheater Eisenach.

In 2016, he was accepted into the German Academy of Performing Arts.

Since the 2018/19 season, he has been working as a dramaturg at the Staatstheater Mainz, but also continues to work as a freelance director (*Madame Bovary*, RLT Neuss 2024). He is responsible for the *Literarisches Quartett* series and works as a translator. He is also a guest lecturer and author, including for the FAZ. With the group Maier Motzki Schärf, he also performs as a reciter and, together with Istvan Vincze, runs the podcast *Playspotting* about drama.

Dalilah Hamam is an assistant director. She has been working at Staatstheater Mainz since 2024.

Prior she studied theatre studies and art history at the Johannes Gutenberg-Universität in Mainz, and graduated with a bachelors degree in 2024.

She assisted several theatre productions, such as Hannah Frauenrath's *Magic Town*, Wolfgang Menardi's *Opening Night* and Milena Mönch's *Connemara*.

She is an ongoing member of the jury for the Plug&Play festival at Staatstheater Mainz – a festival supporting upcoming directors and theatre groups.

In 2025 she developed the autofictional collage *ROOTS* about the racialization of hair together with the actress Flora Egbonu in a residency project at Staatstheater Mainz.

Róisín Daly is a playwright and dramaturg.

Róisín was the winner of Scripts Ireland in 2025 with her play *The Waves Have Ears Too*. She is currently the playwright in residence at Birr Theatre and Arts Centre for 2026. She studied an MA in Dramaturgy at the University of Amsterdam, and holds a BA in English and Drama from Trinity College Dublin.

Róisín served on the reading panel for *The Navigator Project* and for the Fishamble New Writing Award as part of Dublin Fringe Festival 2025.While in the Netherlands, she was involved in establishing a professional association for dramaturgs (MoMo), and worked as a reviewer and researcher with Holland Festival and the Dutch National Opera for the 2025 Opera Forward Festival.

Róisín has completed an internship within the Abbey Theatre's New Work and Literary Department, and first worked with Fishamble as an intern in 2023.

Laura MacNaughton has worked in the professional arts sector for over twenty years in theatre, film and dance. She has worked primarily as a General Manager, Producer and Programmer. Laura has worked at a senior level in multiple arts organisations, these include the Gate Theatre, Dublin Dance Festival and The O'Reilly Theatre. Laura is a drama facilitator and director with Belvedere College Drama Department. Director credits include *Sherlock* (2024) *Bringing Down The House* (2025) and *HOPE SPRINGS* (2026).

Laura currently sits on the Producers Working Group for the Performing Arts Forum. She holds a Science Degree from Trinity College Dublin and is a classically trained musician and Associate of Trinity College London in music performance.

Laura is the Producer at Fishamble: The New Play Company and previous Fishamble credits include *In Two Minds* (2023), *Taigh/Tŷ/Teach* (2024) *BREAKING* (2024), *The Black Wolfe Tone* (2025) and *The Leap* (2025).

Jörg Vorhaben was born in Hamburg and studied theater studies, sociology, and education in Erlangen, Berlin, and Amsterdam. During his studies, he worked as an assistant director at the Maxim Gorki Theater Berlin and co-organized ARENA – International Week of Young Theater in Erlangen.

In the 1999/00 season, he was assistant dramaturg at Schauspiel Hannover, from 2000 to 2002 dramaturg at the Nationaltheater Mannheim, and from 2002 to 2006 dramaturg at Schauspiel Köln. At these theaters, he worked with K.D. Schmidt, Albrecht Hirche, Niklaus Helbling, Friederike Heller, and Sebastian Baumgarten, among others. From 2006 to 2014, he was senior dramaturg at the Oldenburg State Theater and director of the Go West Theater Festival from Flanders and the Netherlands.

Since the 2014/15 season, he has been chief dramaturg at the Staatstheater Mainz. He was dramaturg for the productions *Ramstein Airbase – Game of Drones* (director: Jan-Christoph Gockel), *Sleepless* (director: Hannah Barker), *All das Schöne* (director: Jana Vetten), *ForsterHuberHeyne* (director: ensemble and Peter Van de Eede), and *Drei Mal die Welt* (director: Jan Neumann), among others.

Katharina Greuel studied theater studies and cultural anthropology in Mainz and Lisbon. In addition to working as an assistant director in Germany and Switzerland, she organised local festivals and major events during her studies, including the youth political Open Ohr Festival Mainz. At the Staatstheater Wiesbaden, she was involved in various capacities in all editions of the theater biennial NEUE STÜCKE AUS EUROPA (New Plays from Europe), most recently in 2014 as artistic director of the final festival edition. In the same position, Katharina Greuel organized and directed the International Büchner Festival in Giessen in 2013. At the Institut Français Mainz, she took over the management of the cultural department together with the directorate in 2015, where she was responsible for the artistic program as well as production management and public relations.

In 2021, she moved to the Staatstheater Mainz for the TANZKONGRESS 2022 – SHARING POTENTIALS, where she was responsible for international artistic production as part of the management team.

Since the 2022/23 season, she has been co-directing the Mainz Residenz at the Staatstheater Mainz with Jörg Vorhaben and curating and managing the PLUG&PLAY Theaterfestival für junge Regie (PLUG&PLAY Theater Festival for Young Directors), which she co-founded.

Eoin Kilkenny is a freelance Production Manager mainly focusing on touring. This will be his 14th show with Fishamble stretching back 10 years!

As a long term collaborator of Dan Colley he has toured Dan's work across the world including *Lost Lear*.

He has worked at some of the world's best festivals such as Edinburgh Festival Fringe, Galway International Arts Festival, Melbourne International Arts Festival, and toured work to over 15 countries.

Eoin was honored to work at some special events including the State Visit by HM Queen Elizabeth II, Visit of Pope to Dublin, 1916 centenary celebrations and 2012 Olympic Games.

He trained as a production manager with the Rough Magic SEEDs programme, working on their productions in Dublin, Belfast and New York. He is a product of UCD Dramsoc and has completed a MA in Producing at The Royal Central School of Speech and Drama. For more information please visit eoinkilkenny.com

Niels Sonnemann was born and raised in Frankfurt am Main, and is a husband, father, and grandfather of six. After completing his apprenticeship as a master carpenter and studying interior design, he worked as a carpenter, model maker, and in trade show construction; he built electric guitars in Kenya and worked with the homeless until he found his way into the theater world through the English Theatre in Frankfurt. He came to Mainz in 2020 via the Nationaltheater Mannheim. Since the beginning of the year, he has been the workshop manager at the Staatstheater mainz

Emily Waters is a Limerick based Stage Manager for theatre. Recent credits include Jilly Morgan's *Birthday Party National Tour* (Lime Tree Theatre), *What are You Afraid Of?* At Kilkenny Arts Festival (Rough Magic), Pat Kinevane's *Silent, Forgotten, Underneath, Before* and *KING* for Fishamble as well as previous work with The Abbey Theatre, THISISPOPBABY, Gúna Nua, Catherine Young Dance Co. & Sunday's Child.

Lisa Passow was born in Neuenbürg in 1982 and studied German language and literature, philosophy, and theater studies in Düsseldorf and Mainz. In 2016, she began working at the Staatstheater Mainz as a prompter and assistant director, and now serves as stage manager.

Archer Bradshaw is chief LX and touring relighter in theatre and dance, based in Dublin, Ireland. He is a graduate from The Lir Academy with a BT in Stage Management and Technical Theatre, where he specialised in lighting.

Since graduating, Archer has worked as a Chief LX, Relighter and Programmer with Fishamble on many of their productions, including *Heaven, The Leap* and *KING* across Ireland, India, New York and the UK. Archer frequently works on multi-sensory theatre for young audiences, with and without additional needs, and he is a strong believer in making high-quality work for our younger audiences.

Susanne Pohl, born in Mainz in 1983, studied American Studies, English, and Philosophy at Johannes Gutenberg University Mainz and earned her master's degree.

Since 2017, she has been creating surtitles for various productions at the Staatstheater Mainz, where she has worked as a prompter for the theater since the 2023–24 season.

Evie McGuinness is the Assistant Producer for Fishamble: The New Play Company. Her previous work with the company includes *The Black Wolfe Tone, The Leap* and *The Navigator Project*. She is Line Producer for Brokentalkers covering their international touring in 2025 and 2026 as well as new production *The Mirror Stage*. She has worked as a stage manager for theatre for the last ten years. She graduated with a distinction from The Lir Academy's Stage Management and Technical Theatre course in 2016. She has worked as a stage manager with The Abbey, the Gate Theatre, Landmark Productions, Rough Magic, Pan Pan, Collapsing Horse, The Local Group, Brokentalkers, THISISPOPBABY and Livin' Dred both nationally and internationally. Her previous stage management work includes *MASTERCLASS* by Brokentalkers (Dublin Fringe Festival, Edinburgh Fringe Festival, RISING Festival, Sydney Theatre Festival), *A Very Old Man With Enormous Wings* by Dan Colley (Edinburgh Fringe Festival, National Tour, Imaginate, Auckland Arts Festival) and *Lost Lear* by Dan Colley (Dublin Theatre Festival, National Tour, Aotearoa Festival).

Allie Whelan is the Marketing, Outreach and Engagement Manager at Fishamble: The New Play Company. Allie has worked on *Mustard, King, The Humours of Bandon, In Two Minds, Breaking, Outrage, Heaven, Fight Night, The Black Wolfe Tone, The Leap, The Navigator Project, Refuge* and *For Dolores* with Fishamble.

Allie Whelan graduated from Trinity College Dublin in 2018 with a first class honours degree in Drama & Theatre Studies. Since then she has worked in marketing, communications and social media roles with Dublin Fringe Festival (2021–24), Poetry Ireland, Landmark Productions (*Straight to Video, Walking with Ghosts, Ulysses 2.2,* and *Krapp's Last Tape*), Pan Pan (*The Sudden, The Patient Gloria, The First Bad Man, Cascando* and *History Play*), Glass Mask Theatre (*Describe the Night, Country Music, Mother and Child* and *Celebrity*), The RDS Visual Art Awards (2021-2024) and Music Network Ireland (2022-2023 Spring Touring Season).

Allie has also directed a number of productions, *Pool (No Water)* by Mark Ravenhill, winner of Best Production, Best Ensemble and Best Sound Design at ISDA 2018, *By the Bog of Cats* for Kildare Youth Theatre and *The Terms and Conditions of Me and My Ma* by Conor Burke in 2019.

As well as her work with Fishamble, Allie also works as a designer, photographer and occasionally as a chef.

Sarah Bragg-Bolger is the General Manager for Fishamble: The New Play Company. She is originally from Canada. She is also currently Executive Director of Dublin Youth Theatre where she has produced shows such as *this is a room...* (Dublin Theatre Festival), *The Spanish Tragedy* by Thomas Kyd (the Project Arts Center), *UBU* devised with CN Smith from the Alfred Jarry text (Smock Alley) and co-produced *Sleepwalkers* (Dublin Theatre Festival) with PanPan. She is an associate producer on *The 24 Hour Plays: Dublin* and was formerly the Chair of Youth Theatre Ireland's board of directors.

Previous arts and stage management work include the Lambert Puppet Theatre and the Gate Theatre (Dublin), Shakespeare's Globe (London), Edinburgh International Festival and the Traverse Theatre (Edinburgh), and the Art Gallery of Ontario and the Toronto International Film Festival (Toronto).

Eva Scanlan is the Executive Director at Fishamble: The New Play Company.

Formerly producer at Fishamble, recent productions include *Fight Night* by Gavin Kostick (2025), *Taigh/Tŷ/Teach*, a trilingual co-production with partners in Scotland and Wales (2024), *In Two Minds* by Joanne Ryan (2023), *Heaven* by Eugene O'Brien (2022), *Outrage* by Deirdre Kinahan (2022), *Duck Duck Goose* by Caitríona Daly (2021), *The Treaty* by Colin Murphy (2021), *Embargo* by Deirdre Kinahan (2020), *The Alternative* by Michael Patrick and Oisín Kearney (2019), *Rathmines Road* by Deirdre Kinahan (2018), *On Blueberry Hill* by Sebastian Barry (2017-2021), *Inside The GPO* by Colin Murphy (2016) and Fishamble's award-winning plays by Pat Kinevane *King, Before, Silent, Underneath* and *Forgotten*, and many other productions on tour in Ireland and around the world.

Eva produced *The 24 Hour Plays: Dublin* at the Abbey Theatre in Ireland (2012–26), in association with *The 24 Hour Plays, New York* as a fundraiser for Dublin Youth Theatre. She has worked on *The 24 Hour Plays* on Broadway and *The 24 Hour Musicals* at the Gramercy Theatre in New York. Previously, she was Producer at terraNOVA Collective in New York (2012–15) and has worked on theatre productions, events and conferences at the Bushwick Starr, 59E59 Theaters, New Ohio Theatre, the New School, the Park Avenue Armory, and Madison Square Garden.

All Sie Geist
Refuse
Mainz

REFUGE

Deirdre Kinahan

*For my brother
Hughie Kinahan.
One of Ireland's emigrant hearts.*

Introduction
Jim Culleton, director

Deirdre Kinahan has a wonderful ability to capture the struggles and dilemmas that reflect the times in which we live, and to create characters and tell a story through rich dialogue and visceral energy that reveals the vulnerabilities and complexities of life.

Fishamble has had such rewarding experiences working with Deirdre over the past fifteen years, including her tiny play *Broken* which was part of *Tiny Plays for Ireland* in Dublin, New York, and Washington, DC; *Spinning* which opened at the Dublin Theatre Festival; *Rathmines Road* which was a co-production with the Abbey Theatre; and her two plays for Fishamble during the Decade of Centenaries – *Embargo* about the arms embargo of 1921, and *Outrage* about the Civil War in 1922, each staged one hundred years after the events, at Dublin Port. I directed four of these five productions (*Embargo* was directed by Maisie Lee), and Deirdre is just the kind of playwright that is an absolute pleasure to work with. She has a strong vision about the story she is telling, she is clear-sighted and focused, and yet she also enjoys the collaborative nature of theatre and how playwriting requires a mixture of solitary writing, as well as communal development and rehearsal. She's open to all suggestions and, in fact, embraces ideas by other members of the team, but she knows what she wants to say, and she is brave and fearless in how she does so.

Jörg Vorhaben, a dramaturg at Staatstheater Mainz, saw *Rathmines Road* at the Abbey and commissioned a German version of the play, which was produced in Mainz. He then had the idea of creating a play about a very unique link between Ireland and Germany. He spoke to Deirdre about the Palatine community in Germany which fled religious persecution in 1710 and was brought by Queen Anne to form a community in

Rathkeale, County Limerick. The story seemed like an exciting prospect and both Deirdre and Staatstheater Mainz, under the artistic directorship of Markus Müller, asked Fishamble if we would like to partner with them on the project. We were thrilled to do so, as we are always looking for ways to create new plays that help us grapple with the complicated world in which we live.

Even though the play is inspired by the events of over three hundred years ago, it feels so contemporary, as it explores the characters' journey, as refugees, escaping danger and seeking somewhere safe to live. This is something that's repeated in history too often and which we continue to witness today, so it has been a privilege to work on this play which helps us navigate those stories. Theatre can help the audience to experience life from someone else's perspective and increase our empathy, and Deirdre is a master of doing both.

I spoke to an Irish friend of mine recently whose descendants had come from that Palatine community, and he said that his grandmother always told him they became very close to the Irish and there were many friendships between the two communities. While this is true to some extent of course, life is more complex than that, and theatre has the ability to hold a number of different perspectives in the same space, with which we can engage. Zabi is escaping danger – just as Hannah and her family are – but he experiences racism and abuse through the rise of right-wing sentiment that generates fear around immigration to justify its own racist agenda. Hannah and Zabi are both escaping danger in their homelands. As Hannah says, 'I didn't come to Ireland to conquer or to steal another family's future… I came here for refuge.' However, in a fascinatingly complex play, we see how the German immigrants were facilitated by Lord Southwell and the British government, and many of them fought with the British against the Irish, becoming implicated in the colonisation of Ireland. We see how people like Peter who flee persecution in their own land can themselves support or become the oppressors, 'with a poisonous view of the Irish natives'. In war, lies are generated in order to create moral justification for atrocities to be committed. While the play explores these thorny issues, it also – as my friend's grandmother said – recognises the love and support that humans show others who are seeking safety and refuge.

This co-production has brought two theatre companies from two countries together, so we can learn from each other, and celebrate with audiences our shared humanity and what connects us in a world of divisions. It has been a pleasure working with the German–Irish team on this production, listening to fantastic tunes from Steve Wickham that bring us on a journey through the cultures and timeframes of the play, discussing with Matt Williamson how the spirit of grief which the dancer represents might emerge from the landscape, and exploring cultural differences and similarities with the fantastic cast and design team from both countries.

I'm so grateful for all the support we've had to make this production happen. Thanks to our wonderful colleagues and friends in Staatstheater Mainz, Culture Ireland, the Irish Embassy in Berlin, the Irish Consulate in Frankfurt, Goethe-Institut, Galway Traveller Movement, the Irish Palatine Heritage Centre in Rathkeale, Don Bosco Care, the Afghan Community and Cultural Association of Ireland, and all those who have helped us bring this story to life.

Author's Note

This play is conceived with a live musician on stage playing an eclectic suite of music with Irish/folk/German/rock influences, specifically written for the play. The musician is a ghostly presence, a spirit of the piece, playing throughout. My good friend Steve Wickham created and performed the music for the premiere performance.

There is also a dance element with a lone contemporary dancer, bringing that fluidity, unique expression and language into the mix. He is also an active member of the cast – a spirit of hurt – at times representing those visibly grieved by the characters or mirroring Zabi as Shadow Boy (Ludwig), just as the play mirrors two worlds/two time periods/various communities and cultural histories. Matthew Williamson was the choreographer and dancer for the premiere performance.

The story of this play in told is one place in 2026: a green space close to the ruins of an old castle in Limerick, Castle Matrix. We are outside on the grass beside ruined old outbuildings and carriage houses. Zabi, the young Afghan boy, is hiding in one of the outbuildings, but the front wall is completely crumbled so we can see in and see him. The play tells us Zabi's story of seeking refuge in Ireland in the present day through his interaction with a ghost, Hannah, who came to Ireland seeking refuge with her family in 1709. Molly is a local woman from the Traveller community who is happy interacting with people from the present day and the many ghosts she encounters in this world. Molly acts as a conduit between the two stories of Zabi and Hannah and the two worlds of the play. This setting is important to both the present and the past; Castle Matrix is the area where the Palatine people settled, the river beside the carriage house where Zabi is found is where Hannah drowned, and it is close to where Ludwig, her son, was murdered.

The play is laid out in beats in reflection of the musical element. We move from present day through to the past with fluidity.

The conceit is that Zabi can see the past scenes as acted out through his interaction with Molly and Hannah. The characters Herr Ireland and Peter are ghosts summoned up by Hannah and trapped in a kind of purgatory because she refuses to move on from her sorrow. Ludwig is Hannah's son, he has been waiting for Hannah in the carriage house since the day of his death but she does not see him until a particular moment in her journey through this play.

Refuge is written in English but with slivers of German, Irish and Pashto to reflect the languages spoken by the characters in their day and their time.

D.K.

AOSDÁNA

Characters

HANNAH
MOLLY
HERR IRELAND
PETER
ZABI
SHADOW BOY

Notes

Once a character arrives on stage, they do not leave until the story is told, only the Shadow Boy seems to appear/disappear.

Where a line is delivered in Pashto, Irish Gaelic or German, the language is indicated at the beginning of the line. All other lines should be delivered in English.

/ is overlapping dialogue.

… is a hesitation.

This text went to press before the end of rehearsals and so may differ slightly from the play as performed.

Beat One

Present.

A dance piece – music 'Old Town' by Phil Lynott – and a cacophony of other notes and voices and dissonant screeches and sounds that signify an attack by right-wing activists on a small group of refugees – shouts of:

VOICES. Ireland for the Irish!/Ireland is full!/There's one over there!/Get him!/Out! Out! Out!/We don't want you here!/Go home!

> *A young Afghan man and his friends are being attacked by a group of right-wing activists: he is stunned at first… then runs… keeps running… boards a bus to anywhere… then walks… a long road then turns off into the woods… in the woods he finds an old castle… he crawls into an old carriage shed exhausted… (The energy under the dance should be fear/strange town/panic/running/holing up like a wounded child.)*

Beat Two

Present.

ZABI is sleeping fitfully near the entrance of an old carriage shed of Castle Matrix, Rathkeale, County Limerick. HANNAH, a woman with long red hair, appears out of the gloom. She is wearing early-eighteenth-century peasant dress. She leans in over the young man, tenderly moving his hair out of his eyes. He doesn't wake. She feels his brow. Sits beside him and starts to slowly rock him while humming an old German folk song.

SHADOW BOY – *Ludwig – appears and watches her but she does not see him.*

Another woman, MOLLY, *arrives to the door of the shed, she takes in the scene.*

MOLLY. Is that him?

HANNAH (*in German*). Yes.

MOLLY. How long has he been here?

HANNAH. Two days.

I think he is ill. He doesn't eat.

MOLLY *moves in closer, knocking against an old tin bucket which makes a racket.* ZABI *wakes up with a start, jumps up and retreats into the shed – terrified.*

MOLLY (*to* ZABI). It's okay! I'm sorry it's okay… I didn't mean to frighten you.

ZABI *has taken a rusty cutlery knife from his pocket and flashes it at her…*

What class of a knife is that?

What do you plan to do with it?

Butter me?

ZABI *doesn't answer.*

He just tries to scuttle back into the darkness.

Are you hurt?

HANNAH (*in German*). Are you hurt?

He doesn't answer.

MOLLY. Do you speak English?

He doesn't answer.

Do you speak at all?

He doesn't answer.

I brought food.

Are you hungry?
You must be hungry?

HANNAH (*in German*). You must be hungry?

MOLLY *takes a packet of sandwiches from her backpack and offers them to ZABI. He doesn't move.*

There's soup too, it's hot.

Eat, you must eat.

He still doesn't move.

MOLLY. Jesus, what happened to you?

Why are you here?

HANNAH. Why are you here?

(*In German.*) Why are you here?

HANNAH *repeats the phrase as she spins into a scene from her past.*

Beat Three

Past.

There is the sound of water. The sound of a great river running fast.

It is spring 1710, HANNAH *bends with a small tin cup into the water.*

When she stands she shrieks at the sight of an Irish man standing watching her.

HANNAH (*in German*). Why are you here?

HERR IRELAND. Why are you here?

HANNAH. What are you saying?

HERR IRELAND. Why do you scream?

HANNAH. I just want water. I need water to clean my foot.
I cut my foot. I'm…
Who are you? Are you one of the Papists?

HERR IRELAND. I'm here to fish.

HANNAH. What is the language that you speak?

It is not English?

HERR IRELAND (*in Irish Gaelic*). Fish.

He points to the water and makes a fish movement with his hands.

HANNAH. Ah! Fish. You are here to fish.

She makes the same movement with her hands. They both smile, a little nervous.

HERR IRELAND. You are one of Southwell's Palatines?

HANNAH. You know Lord Southwell?

HERR IRELAND. What is the language that you speak?

It isn't English?

HANNAH. Does he let you fish here?

HERR IRELAND. They say that you're all from the German Nation.
Palatinate?

HANNAH halts, it is the first word she can understand beyond the name Southwell. She points to herself.

HANNAH. Palatine.

She points to him.

Ireland?

He nods.

HERR IRELAND. Ireland!

HANNAH. Well, I have cut my foot, Herr Ireland, and I need to fix it so that I can walk home.

She slips off her clog. H IRELAND *watches intently. She pours the water onto her foot,*

HERR IRELAND. Are they wooden shoes? Wooden shoes! Have you ever seen the like?!

H IRELAND *then tears* a *bit of cloth from his white shirt and offers it to her for* a *bandage.* HANNAH *hesitates but then takes the cloth to tie around her foot.*

I'd say they're hell to walk in, are they?
Wooden shoes!

HANNAH. What is it that you say?

O… (*Taking the cloth.*) Thank you, thank you.

HERR IRELAND. And this…

He hands her a small bunch of herbs from his bag.

She looks confused.

So he indicates rubbing them on her foot.

She follows – rubbing the herbs onto the cut and then tying the cloth around the wound.

HANNAH. You… you are very kind.

Beat Four

Present.

MOLLY (*to* ZABI). Can you see her?

Can you see Hannah?

ZABI *shakes his head.*

I think you understand well what I'm saying.
If you see her, then you are close to death?
Why are you close to death?
Were you thinking of drowning yourself?

ZABI *looks away.*

Well, you haven't a chance now, my friend.
Not here.
Hannah patrols these waters
Hannah's got a better record on the River Deel than the civil
defence itself! She is notorious in these parts.
The ghost with the red hair.

HANNAH *smiles and takes a bow.*

HANNAH (*in German*). The ghost with the red hair!

MOLLY. She came from Germany with her people centuries
    ago. Fleeing war.
    Now she pulls many a broken heart from the river, many
    a broken soul.
    Do you want to know her story?

He doesn't answer.

HANNAH (*in German*). My story?

MOLLY. Or can you see her story too? See it like a robe of
    darkness around her? We all wear our stories, don't we?

HANNAH (*in German*). We all wear our stories, don't we?

MOLLY. Hannah first met Herr Ireland on a spring day.

HANNAH. I first met Herr Ireland on a spring day.
    It was not long after we arrived to Ireland, when all was still
    work and worry and wonder in the green wet wilderness of
    it. *Herr Ireland* was a poacher –

MOLLY. Herr Ireland was a healer and a poacher.

HANNAH. There wasn't a rabbit or a grouse or a salmon safe,
    despite Lord Southwell's guns and the two poacher-catchers
    hired to keep the Irish and their hunger off this estate.

MOLLY. Herr Ireland was her friend.

HANNAH (*in German*). Herr Ireland was my friend.
    Herr Ireland was my secret.
    It was he who brought me here, to this very place to find
    Ludwig.

He who took me from the river.
He who understood me most of all.

HERR IRELAND (*in Irish Gaelic*). I first met the lady Palatine on a spring day.

MOLLY. Herr Ireland first met the lady Palatine on a spring day.

HERR IRELAND. It was not long after she and her kind arrived here, when we were all still in a worry and a wonder as to what their arrival might mean.

MOLLY. Lord Southwell and the English Governors in Dublin gifted each Palatine family with a musket and each Palatine family with a poisonous view of the Irish natives.

HERR IRELAND. So when they arrived here, they didn't pay us the time of day. They didn't trade. They didn't learn our language or our music but turned full square into the bosom of their English benefactors, singing their Protestant hymns, preaching their Protestant tales so as to make a new world out of our world to resemble the German world they had left behind.
But the lady Palatine was different.

MOLLY. Hannah was different.

HERR IRELAND. When she walked the river delivering eggs to her kinsfolk, the lady Palatine spoke to me.
The lady Palatine saw me.
She didn't pretend that we Irish somehow didn't live here, didn't belong. No. She asked me the names of our hills and our flowers and our waters in our own tongue.

HANNAH *points to mushrooms.*

Past.

HANNAH (*in German*). Bluebell?

HERR IRELAND (*in Irish Gaelic*). Bluebell.

HANNAH (*in Irish Gaelic*). Bluebell.

HANNAH (*in German*). Garlic?

HERR IRELAND (*in Irish Gaelic*). Garlic.

HANNAH (*in Irish Gaelic*). Garlic.

HERR IRELAND. The lady Palatine was my friend.
The lady Palatine was my secret – she had to be because
my own people grew to despise the likes of her like they
despised the English for taking all that had once been ours.

Beat Five

Past/present.

PETER *arrives and stands as if on* a *soapbox in early
eighteenth-century London. He may be accompanied by the*
MUSICIAN/DANCER *to help build the notion of this moment
in the past of their story. (This text is actually from* a *letter
written by the Palatines to Queen Anne.)*

PETER. PEOPLE OF LONDON! PEOPLE OF LONDON!
I HAVE A LETTER FOR THE QUEEN'S MOST
EXCELLENT MAJESTY! THE MOST HUMBLE
PETITION BY FIVE HUNDRED AND TWELVE HERE.
FIVE HUNDRED AND TWELVE MADE MISERABLE
BY WAR! FIVE HUNDRED AND TWELVE DESTITUTE
AND RUINED GERMAN PROTESTANTS FROM
THE PALATINATE AND NOW ARRIVED AT SAINT
CATHERINE'S…

MOLLY. London.

ZABI (*in a whisper*). London?

HANNAH. A purgatory. After Mannheim. After Mainz.
After Köln and after Rotterdam. Five hundred and twelve
exhausted refugees camped in tents in the cold heart of
London. After a treacherous journey from home.

ZABI (*in Pashto*). Home.

MOLLY. A terrible journey from river raft to rutted roadside then on to creaking English ships. Nothing to welcome Hannah and her kin at Saint Catherine's but a mere morsel of food, no real shelter or fresh water and little in the way of friendship, despite all the generous offers of resettlement from the English.

HANNAH. I swear I thought at that time that we might be better to return home, devastated as it was, but my husband Peter and the men decided to trust in England's glorious Queen…

PETER. YOUR MAJESTY! WE MISERABLE PEOPLE BEING TOTALLY RUINED BY THE WAR AND OTHER HARDSHIPS GOD THE ALMIGHTY HAS SENT OVER US IN OUR NATIVE COUNTRY, ARE FORCED TO LEAVE OUR HABITATION, OUR KINDRED FRIENDS AND ALL THAT WAS DEAR UNTO US AND TO GO GET OUR LIVELIHOODS IN OTHER PARTS OF THE WORLD.

HANNAH. We waited for weeks.

MOLLY. They waited for weeks.

HANNAH (*in German*). We waited for weeks in St Catherine's.

MOLLY. Weeks of fear and confusion.

HANNAH. As the Queen and her Bishops argued over what was to be done with us. I felt like a stray dog, but finally word came that we were to be settled.

PETER. We are to be settled!

WE ARE SAVED!

(*In German.*) WE ARE SAVED!

He bursts into a rousing hymn – she speaks over him.

HANNAH. Even so, there was not a hymn or argument that could lift the cold or the fear or the homesickness from me as we travelled in our tattered wagons across another sea. Ludwig is all that kept me going. (*When Hannah mentions Ludwig, we see the shadow of a boy flicker across her again.*)

MOLLY. Her son. Her boy.
Ludwig.

HANNAH. Ludwig's young arms tight around my waist.
Ludwig's bright eyes scanning new skies, new hills, new
roads. His heart a great big open door to this adventure.

HERR IRELAND. Ludwig, the little man, the little *Catach*
[curly-haired one] I saw with her always in the early days, in
the woods, along the roads, the little curly head bobbing by
her side, the hand tight in hers.

PETER. AND WHEN WE WERE INFORMED OF YOUR
MAJESTY'S GREAT CLEMENCY BESTOWED ON OUR
SUFFERING NEIGHBOURS…

HERR IRELAND. God but he's off again with his poor
Palatines! That was their whinge when they arrived here.
Look at us: 'The Poor Palatines'. Save us, 'The Poor
Palatines'. Good and hardy Palatines they were with their
seeds and their tools and their special dispensations from the
landlords!

MOLLY. The Palatines were well looked after…

HERR IRELAND. They got all the stone and timber they
needed to build their fine dwellings while we, the Irish, were
shifted off the land like rats.

Shifted off our own land like rats – (*In Irish Gaelic.*) and
then tortured by tithes and rents and rules and regulations
designed to thwart us or kill us off entirely.

HANNAH. It wasn't our war.
It was your war with Southwell and his kin.
Your war with the English,
not the Palatine,
not Ludwig,
not me.

HERR IRELAND (*in Irish Gaelic*). I know this, Hannah.
I know this.
So why must we go over it all again?

HANNAH. Over it and over it.
  I have no choice.
  I am locked in it.
  Locked in this grief with no forgiveness and no respite.

HERR IRELAND. It's not right.

MOLLY. It's not right.

HANNAH. I sinned against God.
  I sinned against Peter,
  I sinned against life itself.

MOLLY. Over and over this story.
  When will it end, Hannah?

HANNAH. No matter.
  Can we help this poor boy?

MOLLY. I don't know.
  (*To* ZABI.) Can we help you? I hope so.

Beat Six

Present.

MOLLY (*to* ZABI). What is your name?
  What is it that brought you here?

ZABI (*in Pashto*). Like rats.

MOLLY. What are you saying?

HANNAH. What are you saying, my friend?

MOLLY. Was it war that brought you here?

HANNAH (*in German*). Was it war that brought you here?

ZABI (*in Pashto*). Ran off the streets like rats.

MOLLY. Did he say something?

Did you say something?
Why don't you speak to us?
I can't keep trying to reach into your mind to try to figure
you out. It looks like a mess of a mind. Fragments. As much
of a ruin as this old castle. Blown asunder if I read you right.

The SHADOW BOY *appears and there is the sound of
something knocking/banging on the shed.* ZABI *puts his
head into his hands.*

What is it?

HANNAH. It is just the trees, my friend.
Just a branch of the tree banging on the roof.

MOLLY. What is it that haunts you?

HANNAH. It is nothing to be frightened of.

ZABI (*speaking to himself at first in Pashto. Low and
incoherent to the others but not to the audience*). On the
door. On the door. Such a wild knocking on the door.
A great strong knocking on the door. And then my mam
screamed. 'Zabi. Zabi,' she scream and screamed. 'Zabi,
you must come.' But I could not see. I could not see past my
mam so I push and then I saw my father. I see him. I see him
all bloodied and broken in the ground. So many bullets. So
many bloody holes and blood all in the ground. His face is
gone. Just the beard. And all twisted. All wrong. 'Run, run,'
screamed my mam, she says, 'Go get your cousin to help, to
help me, help.'

MOLLY. What did you say?
What did he say?

ZABI (*in Pashto*). My father was in the Taliban.

HANNAH. Taliban?

MOLLY. Did you say something?

HANNAH. He says Taliban.

MOLLY. Does he?
Did he?

Did you say Taliban?

ZABI *shakes his head and shrinks away again.*

HANNAH. He says it in his sleep.
He says Father.
He says Kabul.
Mam.
Uncle.
London.

MOLLY. London?
Have you been to London?

ZABI *shakes his head.*

HANNAH. What is the language that you speak?

ZABI. My mam she gives me shoes. She pack my things. 'It is
cold over there,' she says, 'You must wear these shoes, Zabi.'
I never have these new shoes before.
New shoes mean I must go far but I did not know the truth,
did not know what was happening and my mam she cry and
cry.
Only a boy. I was only a boy.
(*In Pashto.*) Nine years old, and I have to walk and walk,
walk for days.
Days after the taxi to Kabul.

MOLLY. Kabul?

HANNAH. Where is this place?

MOLLY. Have you anyone?
Have you anyone we can contact for you?

HANNAH. He won't answer.
He is too frightened.

MOLLY. We need to get him out of this shed.
Out into the light.
To see if he is hurt.
Won't you come out?
Won't you eat?

You can trust us.
We don't want to hurt you…

ZABI. Irish voices.
Irish voices kicking, spitting, punch…
They look at me, look at us like we are rats…

He shouts out a stream of Pashto curses.

He kicks out from his crouched position. The two women move away.

HANNAH. I think he has a fever.

MOLLY. I think so too, there might be an injury.

HANNAH. He hasn't moved this two days.

MOLLY. Two days? There might be an infection.
We have to try to get him to move or I'll have to go get someone.

HANNAH. Who?

MOLLY. I don't know. A doctor? Police?

HANNAH. But what if he is in trouble?
No, no Molly, we must help him, we must try to coax him out.

HANNAH repeats 'Coax him. Coax him out,' as she spins back into another scene from her past.

Beat Seven

Past.

PETER. Hannah! Hannah!

HANNAH. What is it?

PETER. Ludwig has hidden himself in the barn again.

HANNAH. What?

PETER. I was driving in the cattle and they frightened him.

HANNAH. So?! Can't you coax him out?

PETER. He says he will only come out for Mama.
    I am afraid you have him soft.

HANNAH. And I am afraid you have him tormented with your
    building and your herding and your constant instruction.

PETER. We all have to work!

HANNAH. Ludwig is only a boy.
    He is far from home.
    Why not let him play with the Switzer and the Leager boys.

PETER. The devil makes work for idle hands.

HANNAH. The boy is only six!

PETER. We need to show Lord Southwell that we Palatine are
    here to work.

    That we Palatine are here to tame this wilderness… That /

HANNAH. So is Lord Southwell in our barn?

    Is Lord Southwell in our fields or in our kitchen when you
    push and push and push poor Ludwig to dig or mend or hoe?

PETER. Ludwig likes to work.

HANNAH. Ludwig likes to please you, Peter, but you need to
    let him play, play with the other boys sometimes, you need to
    let him be a child.

PETER. I want… /

HANNAH (softer). I know what you want. I know, I know…
    Shhhh.

PETER. There has been enough hunger, Hannah.
    There has been enough death.

HANNAH. I know. I know that more than most.

PETER. I really believe we have a chance here.
    The land is good.
    The soil is rich enough to grow anything…

HANNAH. I know.
  You say it every day.

PETER. With our hands, in our hands, Hannah… We can build
  paradise. We are not like the Irish, they waste this land, they
  have laid waste to it for decades with their pig and potato.
  We are different. We… /

HANNAH. Why are you preaching, Peter?
  There is no congregation here.
  There are none of Southwell's men here.
  It is only me. You are speaking only to me.
  And you have nothing to prove to me.

PETER (*quietly*). You won't… We won't lose another son. ·

HANNAH. Shhhh… I know…

PETER. You will be safe here.
  Ludwig will grow up to be a man.

  She embraces him.

  That's why I work the way I do…

HANNAH. I know, I know, shhhh…

PETER. I want… I don't want… Never again, Hannah…
  I need Ludwig to be strong…

HANNAH. He is. He will be.
  We just need to coax him out of your barn…

  They laugh a little, stand and sway in their embrace. The
  SHADOW BOY *once again flickers by.*

  Present.

MOLLY. Hannah knew Peter all of her life. She knew him since
  they walked through the vineyards to and from school. Her
  father worked with Peter's father. Her mother baked with
  Peter's mother. Both families were so happy to see them
  make a match.

PETER. Vineyards of home…

HANNAH. Lines and lines of vine basking in the midday sun.

PETER. The Palatinate.

HANNAH. Heavy with fruit.
Heavy with summer.
Marching up to our colourful timber houses from the mouth
of the Rhine.

PETER. The Rhine.
A real river.
A majestic river.
The sight of it never to be matched in Ireland.

HANNAH. I never wanted to leave…

MOLLY. Hannah never wanted to leave.

HANNAH. But Peter's eyes grew full of gold.

MOLLY. Full of gold.

PETER. A book of gold!

MOLLY. A book that went racing through their small German
villages on feet of promise!

HANNAH. Feet of lies!

PETER. The new world, Hannah!

HANNAH. The new world?

PETER. It says it here in the book of gold!
Free land.
Free food.
No French or Spanish soldiers stealing our grain, our cattle,
our wine.
It says it here in the book of gold!
There is a new world, vast and empty!
Free land! Free houses! Free horses!
And riches beyond our wildest dreams.

HANNAH. But it was lies.

PETER. Carolina!

HANNAH. Palatinate.

PETER. America! New York! The New World!

HERR IRELAND. So how the hell did ye end up in Limerick?

HANNAH. A twist of fate, Herr Ireland.

MOLLY. A whim, a notion of auld England's Queen!

PETER. A Protestant people for a Protestant kingdom.
    This is what she says, this Queen.
    Ireland.

HERR IRELAND. But Ireland wasn't empty.

HANNAH. I came here like a ghost, Herr Ireland.
    I came here like I was sleepwalking.
    You know that.
    It was only Ludwig that kept me breathing.

MOLLY (*to* ZABI *who is watching the story unfold*). What is it
    that keeps you breathing?
    There must be someone somewhere out there looking for
    you?
    Someone who needs to know that you are here?

HERR IRELAND. I could see from the first that there was
    a melancholy about her, about my lady Palatine. And I could
    see the ghost of another little lad hanging about her. I could
    see him in her eyes.

HANNAH. Albert.

PETER. Albert.

HANNAH. Born into a cold cold winter.
    A winter he could not survive.

MOLLY. Buried in the hard ground of Germany when her world
    was all but frozen.

HANNAH. Albert.

PETER. Albert.
    Will you never forgive me for the loss of him, Hannah?
    After all of it?

HERR IRELAND. It near killed her to leave that little body
    behind.

Beat Eight

Present.

HANNAH *comes and sits beside* ZABI *again.*

HANNAH. Where is your home, *Catach*?
Where is home?
Is it Kabul?

MOLLY. You can tell us, you can trust us, son.

HANNAH. You got some soup into him?!

MOLLY. I did.

HANNAH. Good boy.

MOLLY. Good boy is right!
Sure he must have been starved.
You must have been starved, son!
Now won't you tell us where you've come from?
And come out into the sunshine?
Come on, take my hand.

MOLLY *puts out her hand.*

HANNAH *puts out her hand.*

HANNAH (*in German*). Take my hand.

MOLLY. Come on, *Catach.*

ZABI. My hand. My hand. The Taliban men they take my
hand. The men they lift the axe. I scream. I pull. It is only
my finger that's blood, blood, bloody, all blood but it still
there… It is not come away. Laughing. They laugh. The
Taliban men. They take another boy. I scream. I fall into the
ground like my father. I think that this is my last day. I pray
to God.
I pray.

MOLLY. It's all right.
Why not come outside and tell us?
Outside where we can hear you right.

HANNAH. Molly only wants to help you, *Catach*.

ZABI. But I am not myself. I cannot be myself for days when
the Taliban kidnap me. I am afraid that I will never go home
again. But then my cousin comes and they say to him – the
Taliban – they say:
'Zabi, he must stay with us or you must pay.'
'Zabi, he must stay with us because his father is dead.'
'Zabi will fight now in the place of his father.'
So my cousin, he comes again and he pays the Taliban men.
My cousin comes, he gets me free.

MOLLY (*still reaching out her hand*). Come.

HANNAH (*still reaching out her hand*). Come.

MOLLY. Is there someone looking for you?
Come on, son. Come outside.
We are not going to hurt you.

ZABI *slowly begins to shuffle out of the shed.*

The SHADOW BOY *arriving with him.*

ZABI *and the* SHADOW BOY *appear to sit side by side.*

Beat Nine

Present.

PETER. Hurt.
I hurt the ones that I love, loved most in my life.
I hurt you, Hannah.
I am sorry.

HANNAH. I know.

PETER. I knew Hannah since I was a boy.
And I loved Hannah since I was a boy.
Hannah's brown arms. Hannah's clever smile and Hannah's
hair the colour of the sunset.

ZABI. Hannah.

PETER. Hannah walked with us to school.
    Hannah's head held high like a count or a queen.

    She told us stories of *Rumpelstilzchen und Loreley* as we
    traipsed through vine and stoney river roads, trying to keep
    up with her long strides, utterly in thrall to her lilt and her
    shine.

MOLLY. Peter determined to marry Hannah from the age of six.

PETER. I determined to marry Hannah from the age of six.
    I just had to wait to grow up.

HANNAH. Peter.

PETER. I love you, Hannah.
    Loved you.

HANNAH. I know.

PETER. Please forgive me.
    Come back to me.
    It is time.

    But HANNAH *turns away from him and back to the story.*

HANNAH (*to* ZABI). I knew Peter since I was a girl.
    I knew Peter loved me since I was a girl.
    And I knew that he was honest.
    I knew that he was kind.
    I knew that he would work hard to make a life for us,
    hard to make me happy.

PETER. We were happy once?

HANNAH (*turning to* PETER). Yes, we were happy once.

PETER. But then I lost you.
    We lost you.
    Come back to me. Please?!

Beat Ten

Past/present.

HERR IRELAND. I wanted to speak to her. I wanted to speak to my lady Palatine in her own language so I stole one of their Bibles from a bellicose fat little fella called Geyer that rode around Limerick on the most unfortunate-looking horse.

HANNAH. Pastor Geyer!

HERR IRELAND. Calling out to all and sundry about the glory of his God and the evils of Papist living, Papist cursing and Papist poitín. I'll tell you, you could hardly see the man for sanctimony and hymn books, so I'd say he hardly missed it.

HERR IRELAND *comes over to* HANNAH *with the hymn book behind his back.*

(*In atrocious German.*) Hail, O Blessed One, the Lord be with you!

HANNAH. What?

HERR IRELAND (*to himself*). God but it's a guttural fast-paced leap of a thing, this German.

HANNAH. What do you say?

HERR IRELAND (*to himself*). How do you make it sound so gentle on your lips?

HANNAH. I don't understand?

HERR IRELAND. Right so. I'll go again!
(*In German.*) Hail, O Blessed One, the Lord be with you!
The Lord is with you.

HANNAH. The Lord is with me?
What is this?

HERR IRELAND. God is love!
Let the fields be jubilant!

HANNAH *laughs, she looks behind his back.*

HANNAH. What is this you are saying?
What have you behind your back?

HERR IRELAND *tries to keep the book hidden, they kind of dance around each other, then she quickly snatches it from him!*

A Bible?!

You read the Bible?

HERR IRELAND. I do!

HANNAH. In German?

HERR IRELAND. I want to try to talk to you.

HANNAH. What?

HERR IRELAND *indicates his mouth.*

HERR IRELAND. Talk!

HANNAH. But you do talk to me.
You talk to me like the river, like the mountains, like the thrush, and the blackbird.

HERR IRELAND (*in Irish Gaelic*). Blackbird.

HANNAH (*in German*). Blackbird.

(*In German.*) Heron.

HERR IRELAND (*in German*). Heron.

He points to the river.

(*In Irish Gaelic.*) Heron.

HANNAH *looks to the river.*

HANNAH (*in Irish Gaelic*). Heron.

HERR IRELAND. Heron!

HANNAH (*in German*). Why do I always find you alone?

HERR IRELAND. What?

HANNAH. Why do I always find you alone?
Like the heron you stand alone.
Are you alone in the world, Herr Ireland?

HERR IRELAND. What is it you are saying?

HANNAH *smiles.*

HANNAH. Nothing. It is nothing.

He smiles too. There is a moment between them.

HANNAH *walks away.*

Beat Eleven

Past.

HANNAH *is now working in her garden.*

She is humming the Laureley melody.

PETER *is watching, he joins in the singing! She stops.*

PETER. Why do you stop?
Don't… please… it reminds me of home.

HANNAH. That and the sunshine.

PETER *smiles.*

PETER. Yes, that and the sunshine.
Sunshine is rare here.

HANNAH. It is.

PETER. But just look at your garden, Hannah!
It is blooming!
I think it will give us our cider apples this year!

HANNAH. I think so too.

PETER. It is *wunderbar*!
You work so hard.
You make me proud.

He embraces her, humming the tune she was singing, there is a lovely moment between them.

Didn't Alfred Heck do well to bring us those saplings from home. He got them through a merchant in Dublin.

HANNAH. I don't see what is wrong with Irish apples.

PETER. And we are to grow hemp!

HANNAH. Hemp?

PETER. Yes. This is the news.
I have just come from speaking with Alfred, and he has asked me to attend a meeting up at the castle where we will ask Lord Southwell for more land just for this purpose.

HANNAH. More land?

PETER. I am to attend at the castle!
I am to be a part of the council!

HANNAH. I see.

PETER. Aren't you pleased?

HANNAH. Of course… Of course I am pleased.

PETER. We will prosper here, Hannah.
We already prosper.
All of our suffering.
It is over now.

HANNAH. Is it?

PETER (*in German*). Yes, yes it is over now.

HANNAH. Apples and hemp.
They are not the same as people.
Not the same as family.

PETER. I know that, Hannah, and I know how much you miss them but as we prosper we can send for our family! My mother. Your sister…

HANNAH. They will not come!

PETER. They might.

HANNAH. They will not leave home.

Rent more land?
Go to the castle to plead with Lord Southwell?
We have no autonomy here.

PETER. We build our autonomy.
We build it with hard work.

HANNAH. But these low grey skies are not ours, Peter, these
soft hills, they do not belong to us and I cannot pretend,
I will not pretend it is ours or it is home like you do.

PETER. But you like it here?
I thought you liked this Irish landscape, the way you walk in
it for hours.

HANNAH. Yes, I like it.
I like the bogland. I like the rivers.
I like the delicate cotton flower that can be found in the
grasses.
The dark earth,
and the way it splits,
splits as if the world is opening up to speak to us.

PETER. So! Perhaps it is time.

HANNAH. Time?

PETER. For another child?

HANNAH. What did you say?

PETER. Family! You miss family.
So we will make more family!
Family to run with you in your bogland.
Family to fill this fine house.
Family for Ludwig.
A brother for Ludwig!

HANNAH. How can you say that?
How, Peter?
Ludwig has a brother.

PETER. Of course. Of course he does and we will never forget
little Albert… but it has been four years…

HANNAH. I know exactly how long it has been.

PETER. So I think… I hope… that God might bless us now with another child? Bless us now like he does with your garden…

She shakes her head, coming back to the present.

HANNAH. Peter.

PETER (*still in the scene*). Because I love you, Hannah.
I need you, Hannah.

HANNAH *moves out of the scene and comes back to the present and* ZABI.

HANNAH. Peter.
Grasping onto his dreams like a drowning man.
Grasping onto hope. Onto me.
I never did refuse his love, but I knew that no more children would come.
I knew that my womb gave up after Albert.
There was too much pain in the loss of him.
My happiness lay in Ludwig now, not in more children.
And my happiness lay in embracing this strange land of Ireland.
Because this strange land of Ireland put a spell on me.

Beat Twelve

Present.

HERR IRELAND. They were as uniform as a flock of geese in the sky, the Palatine. Uniform in their little half-moon of houses… Their village green, strong gates, commonage and school.
Uniform in their loyalty to the English.
And industrious.
Industrious as a colony of ants they were.
Colonising us.

HANNAH. No, no…

HERR IRELAND. And for all your loveliness, all our
    friendship, Hannah, I knew that you were one of them.
    So I feared for you.
    There could only be trouble in your coming.

HANNAH. Trouble in our coming.
    Trouble I could feel.

HERR IRELAND. Like a stirring underground.

MOLLY. A tremor.
    A gasp.

HERR IRELAND. A lash of anger and indignation blowing up
    like a gas from the boglands beyond.

MOLLY. Houghers.

HERR IRELAND. Houghers.

HANNAH. No!

HANNAH moves away from HERR IRELAND.

The SHADOW BOY *stands up and returns to the shed.*

Only ZABI *seems to see him.*

Present.

ZABI. What trouble?

MOLLY. Trouble, trouble as old as time.

HERR IRELAND *moves away.*

MOLLY *looks to* ZABI.

So what is your trouble, my friend?
    Can you stand up?
    Can you walk?

ZABI *nods his head. He stands up slowly and tentatively
starts to walk around,* MOLLY *watching.*

There!
    Good man.

HANNAH *turns to see him.*

HANNAH. Nothing broken?

MOLLY. No.
    On the outside at any rate.

HANNAH. That is good.

    They watch him slowly walking.

    MOLLY *starts to hum 'Dancing in the Moonlight' by Thin Lizzy.*

    ZABI *stops walking, he is surprised.*

ZABI. Phil Lynott?

MOLLY. Aha!! He speaks!
    Finally he speaks!

HANNAH (*in German*). Thank God.

MOLLY. You were beginning to wear me out.

ZABI. Phil Lynott?

MOLLY. Is that it? Two words?
    Or have you a few more hidden beneath those curls?

    He doesn't answer.

    Do you like Phil Lynott?
    Do you like Irish music?

    She sings a few more bars.

    ZABI *smiles.*

    Well now!

    He speaks, he walks and he smiles!

    MOLLY *and* HANNAH *look to each other!*

MOLLY/HANNAH. Progress!

Beat Thirteen

Past.

HERR IRELAND *approaches* HANNAH*, producing a small pouch of strawberries from the sack he always carries on his shoulder.*

HERR IRELAND (*in Irish*). Strawberries.

HANNAH. Strawberries.

HERR IRELAND *proffers them to her.*

HERR IRELAND. They are for you.

She hesitates. Then she moves back into the scene taking one.

Do you like it?

HANNAH. Of course.
They are sweet.
They are lovely.

HERR IRELAND (*in Irish*). Lovely.

HANNAH (*in Irish*). Lovely.

HERR IRELAND (*in Irish*). I brought you some plants, too.

He presents her with some seedlings in clay and cloth.

HANNAH. O, you brought me some plants too!

(*In Irish.*) Strawberries.
Delicious.
Won't you have one?

HERR IRELAND (*in German*). No, thank you.

HANNAH. Why not?

HERR IRELAND. I like to see you enjoy them.

She proffers again.

HANNAH. Go on, have one.

HERR IRELAND (*shaking his head*). No, no, they hold only bittersweet memories for me.

HANNAH (*in German*). Bittersweet.

HERR IRELAND. They were Áine's favourite thing in the whole wide world.

HANNAH. Áine?

HERR IRELAND. Summer couldn't come quick enough for her and her strawberries.

HANNAH. Áine, was your wife?

HERR IRELAND *puts his hand on his heart.*

(*In Irish.*) Heart.

HERR IRELAND. Yes!
You remember.

HANNAH. I remember.
Áine.
But you so rarely talk of her?

HERR IRELAND. There is little room for talking after grief.
No words, but you know that, Hannah.
(*In German.*) No words.

MOLLY. Áine was Herr Ireland's heart.

HERR IRELAND. Áine.

MOLLY. A beautiful, brave and clever woman.

HERR IRELAND. Taken away from me by a sickness.
Taken by a great pain… Here…

He indicates the lower right side where the appendix is.

HANNAH, *still in the scene, puts her hand on the same place on her right side.*

MOLLY. Such pain.
Ferocious pain.
Ate her up.
Ate her away in only a few days.

HERR IRELAND. One day she was singing, running, kissing,
   cursing…
   The next, she was stricken.

He is visibly upset. HANNAH *reaches out to comfort him.*

   And me?! For all my potions.
   All my blather – I couldn't save her.
   I could do nothing to stop the pain, the wretched pain, the
   fever, convulsions… until a great stillness washed over
   her… just came over her like a wave and her hand, her hand,
   her slender hand… it fell away…

HANNAH (*in Irish*). Hands?

HERR IRELAND (*putting out his hands*). Useless. My hands,
   Hannah.
   Useless!
   All the aches and pains and wounds over the years.
   All the learning, mixing, feeling, finding, healing…
   Since I was a boy, since I was but a boy.
   Yet when it came to my own, comes to my own, I fail, failed,
   failed Áine.

   HANNAH *takes his hands in hers. Examines them.*

HANNAH. Good hands.
   These are good hands…

*Then she lifts one hand up to her face, and caresses her own
cheek with it, surprising them both.*

Beat Fourteen

Present.

MOLLY *turns to* ZABI.

MOLLY. I lost my own brother that way.
   A long time ago.

ZABI. When?

MOLLY. When we were only children.
  Same way.
  Same pain.

She touches her right side.

And I thought I'd never recover.
  Thought I'd just roll myself up in a ball of forgetting like
  you. Or seek peace in the depths of that river.

ZABI. Is that why you see her? See Hannah too?

HANNAH *still in the earlier scene.*

HANNAH. I don't know how I can live this life without you.

HERR IRELAND. Without me? What do you say, Hannah?

HANNAH. I say, I wonder will you leave me too.
  Like Albert.
  Like Ludwig who moves more and more into his father's
  world.

HERR IRELAND. What is it?

HANNAH. Nothing.
  I am happy.
  That's all.

HERR IRELAND. Good.
  (*In German.*) That is good.

Back to MOLLY *and* ZABI.

MOLLY. I see them all, son.
  All the ghosts.
  Always have…

HANNAH (*in German*). All the ghosts.

ZABI (*in Pashto*). Ghosts.

MOLLY. All the spirits and ghouls that cling to this earth
  in rage, disappointment, guilt or grief.

ZABI. But why?

MOLLY. Because the air is thick with them, isn't it?
    Soldiers, Druids, Pagans, Priests.
    Lovers, liars, the murdered, the murdering.
    Broken mothers, absent fathers, lost babes.
    The unbaptised, the forgotten, imprisoned, maligned.
    I see them all.
    Feel their pain in the sting of every drop of rain,
    every howl of thunder or scream of hail.
    Some say it is a gift but I have to ignore them mostly for fear
    I'd go mad myself, for fear that they'd devour me up entirely
    with their hurt and their secrets, their regret and their loss.
    But Hannah is different.
    Hannah never comes to me on her own account.
    Hannah uses her ghost-time here to try to help the living.
    Isn't that right, Hannah?
    The tragedy is that she will not help herself.
    Forgive herself.

ZABI. Forgive? Forgive what?

HANNAH. I took my own life, *Catach.*

MOLLY. Drowned herself not far from here.
    From where she found Ludwig.

ZABI. Ludwig is her son?

MOLLY. Yes.
    Now won't you please tell us who you are.

HANNAH. Who you are, *Catach*?

ZABI. Zabi. I am Zabi.

HANNAH. Zabi, this is your name!

ZABI. But I don't want to go back.

MOLLY. Back where? Kabul?

ZABI. No. No. I am a long time from Kabul.
    I am a long time in Ireland.
    In Dublin.

MOLLY. So is there someone I can contact for you?
  Family?
  Your mother?

ZABI. No, no my mam, she is dead.
  I never see her since I left.

MOLLY. Kabul?

ZABI. A village. My village far from Kabul.
  A long time. I leave a long time ago.
  I had to leave because I was kidnap three times after my
  father was killed.

MOLLY. Kidnapped?

ZABI. And my mam she was scared for me, but she did not
  tell me I was going, so when the taxi came to take me away,
  I think I am only visiting family in Kabul but I am at the
  border with Pakistan and the driver he say to me, 'Go to that
  mountain, Zabi, and run.' He gives me a small gun to fire
  with smoke and colour. When I get to the mountain, I am to
  shoot it and the agent comes.
  'London' he say.
  'You will go to London, Zabi, and work with your uncle.'
  But I never get to London.
  But I hope when I get my passport. My Irish passport. I can
  go. Catriona says then I can go.

MOLLY. Who is Catriona?

  Can I contact Catriona?

ZABI. She is the boss. My worker.

MOLLY. Your social worker?

ZABI. Yes, she help me since I come to Ireland.
  She help me since I come from Calais.

MOLLY. You were in Calais?

ZABI. I was everywhere!
  Walking. Walking. Everywhere.
  Iran.

Italy.
Bulgaria.
Living in rooms.
Waiting in small rooms like prisons.
Sometimes without food.
Many times, many times I thought it was my last day and
I pray to God that I will die but then I remember my mam
and she giving me my shoes so I want to stay alive to get to
London because this is what she wanted.
But then I lose these shoes in Calais.
Too small now. Burst.
After many years of walking.

MOLLY. Lord God.

ZABI. I'm sorry.
Sometimes I am not myself.

MOLLY. Of course.
It's okay. Don't worry.

ZABI. I don't want to go back.
I am tired. So tired.

MOLLY. Don't worry, don't worry.
We will get you fixed up.

HANNAH. You are with friends now.

MOLLY. Friends.

HANNAH (*in Irish*). Friends.

Beat Fifteen

Past.

HERR IRELAND *brings* a *bag of turf to* HANNAH*'s house.*

HANNAH. Thank you. Thank you, Séan.

HERR IRELAND. Will I put it up against the front wall?

HANNAH. Ja, ja, that is perfect.

HERR IRELAND. Remember you need to keep the turf dry –
(*In German.*) dry – or it won't burn.

HANNAH (*In German*). Dry –
(*In English.*) Thank you. I know this.
Peter and Ludwig will put them away with the wood in the
barn later.

HERR IRELAND. Grand, so. I'll be off /

HANNAH. No… no, not yet, Séan.
I have a gift for you –

HERR IRELAND. A gift.

HANNAH (*in Irish*). Yes! Gift.

She rushes into the house to fetch her gift. HERR IRELAND
looks uncomfortable outside the house.

I have made you a shirt.

HERR IRELAND. What?

HANNAH. I have my own spinning machine now…

HERR IRELAND. My God but that's a lovely thing, Hannah…
I cannot accept it.

HANNAH. Why not?
It is a joy for me to make you this gift.

HERR IRELAND. No, no, there is no need.

HANNAH. To thank you for your kindness!

PETER *suddenly arrives and stands aghast at the sight of*
HERR IRELAND.

Peter!

PETER *doesn't answer.*

Herr Ireland, I mean Séan, has brought us more turf.

PETER *continues to stand in silence.*

You liked it so much on the fire last year.

PETER. Hannah, go inside.

HANNAH. What?

PETER. You must go inside right now.

HERR IRELAND. I'll be off.

PETER. Yes. Yes. You will be 'off'… *Schwein.*

HERR IRELAND. What did you say?

HANNAH. Peter!

PETER. You have no right to be here! No permission…

HERR IRELAND. I don't need your fucking permission…

PETER. But you do!
  You Irish are all the same…

HERR IRELAND. I came here to do your wife a service.

PETER. My wife!
Mein Frau! Mein!
So take your eyes off her… and take your filthy hands and
filthy face and thieving ways off back to your bog and your
stinking cabin. *Hexenmeister.*

HERR IRELAND *moves to punch* PETER *but* PETER
quickly picks up an axe and wields it. HANNAH *screams,*
HERR IRELAND *stands his ground.*

HANNAH. No, no, Peter, have you lost your mind?

HERR IRELAND. Take a swing of that and I swear I'll take the
  head off ya!

HANNAH. Go, Séan, go!

PETER. Ja, ja… 'Go Séan go', don't you hear her?
  Don't you hear my wife?

HANNAH. Please…

PETER. You are not wanted here!
    You have no right!

There is another moment of stand-off.

HANNAH. Please, Séan…

    HERR IRELAND *looks at* HANNAH *then turns to leave.*

PETER. That's it. That's it, Irish.
    Get the hell off my farm.

    HERR IRELAND *spits at* PETER*'s feet.*

HERR IRELAND (*in Irish Gaelic*). May the curse of God be on
    you.

    HERR IRELAND *leaves.*

HANNAH. Holy God, Peter!
    What do you think you are doing?

PETER. What do you think YOU are doing?
    To bring that Irish here!

HANNAH. He just brought us some turf!

PETER. I don't want it!

HANNAH. But we trade with them now.
    I thought we trade with them now

PETER. At the market, Hannah.
    In the fields or in the town.
    But we don't bring them here!
    We don't bring the dirty Irish here!
    Onto Lord Southwell's estate!
    Or into our village!
    They don't belong here… and now… of all times… now!
    With all the recent trouble from these Houghers…

HANNAH. Houghers?

PETER. These Irish villains that come to harm us.

HANNAH. But Séan is not here to harm us.
    He is our neighbour.

PETER. *Nein. Nein.* The Switzer. The Leager. The Benner. They
are your neighbour but you pay them less attention than you
do your hens! Don't think I don't notice, don't think our
neighbours don't notice your distance or how you disappear
off into these boglands day after day…

HANNAH. How can you say that?
I work here all the days. I teach at the school in the
mornings. I tend to the garden, the orchard, the house!

PETER. Stop it now.
Stop this screeching and go inside.

HANNAH. No.

PETER. For God's sake, Hannah.
Can't you see that Anna Leager is watching.
It is dangerous. Dangerous what you are doing.
To speak to these Irish. To walk through the country alone.
But you don't listen… Why don't you ever listen?

HANNAH. Because you live in fear, Peter. Because you live in
Lord Southwell's world of fear and gates and suspicion and
walls. I thought we came here to be free.

PETER. No more, Hannah!
I'm telling you, there will be no more speaking with Irish,
you will not bring this shame onto me or onto Ludwig.

HANNAH. Shame?

PETER. These Irish are heathens, Hannah.
These Irish are drunkards.
And now! Now they turn to violence.

HANNAH. What are you talking about?

PETER. Hougher attacks! Irish attacks!
At Ballingarrane. Adare.
When they come in the night!
These Houghers come into our farms at night!
To maim our cattle!
Put fire to our barns!

HANNAH. But Séan is no Hougher.

PETER. All the Irish are Houghers. Don't you see?
They don't want us here. They don't want us here, Hannah,
because they don't understand that this is Lord Southwell's
land now, Lord Southwell's country, not theirs.

HANNAH. Lord Southwell has turned your head.
Turned your head with the little scrap of power he gives you.
You and Alfred Heck and your petty council.

PETER. Lord Southwell keeps us safe.
I'm telling you, Hannah.
I will hear no more from you.
You are to stay inside the house. You are not to speak to this
'Séan' or his Papists and you are never NEVER to bring
them here again. Understood?!

Now I will have to go to Alfred Heck to explain your
mistake.

I just hope that Lord Southwell or his agents don't hear of
this terrible thing.

PETER *leaves.*

HANNAH *sees the shirt she made, all trampled into the
ground.*

She picks it up.

Beat Sixteen

Present.

HERR IRELAND. Terrible thing?
To take a man's home is a terrible thing.
To take a man's language, culture and way of life is a terrible
thing.
You Palatine look at us now like the English do.
You Palatine look at us now like we are dirt.

Beat Seventeen

Present.

ZABI. *'Dirty Arab. Dirty Mozzie. Dirty fuck. Just fuck off
    home.'*
    This is what they say. This is what they scream at me.

MOLLY. Where?

ZABI. Everywhere. Anywhere.
    But…

MOLLY. But what?

ZABI. They never hit before. Attack before.
    So I run.
    Run and run and run into the streets, into the cars, the night,
    that night.

MOLLY. Where was this?
    Where did it happen?

ZABI. Abbey Street. I think.
    Town. I am in town with my friends when they come out of
    a pub, out of the dark and they start their shout.
    We try to turn. We try walk fast but then they trip, they trip
    up my friend Ozcan and he is on the ground and more, more
    now coming, shouting, and we separate but Ozcan can't get
    up, I try to help him get up but now they have me too, have
    me on the ground too… kicking, kicking, kicking… then
    I don't know… something makes them stop… a light…
    for a second, a minute… they stop. And I… I roll, I stand,
    I run…
    I run.
    I run and run and run to a bus.
    It is quiet.
    It is standing at the station.
    The driver, I think he see me as he leaves.
    I know I am bleeding, I know I am dirty,
    but he doesn't say anything.
    He lets me sleep.

MOLLY. Jesus.

ZABI. I don't want any trouble.
    I am in Ireland six year with no trouble.
    I just want to work.
    Get my passport.
    Find my family.

MOLLY. Okay. Okay.
    I understand.
    If you come with me, I can get a doctor,
    I can call Catriona.

ZABI. But what about Ozcan?

    What about my friend? I leave him. I run.

MOLLY. You had to run. You had to save yourself.
    You didn't attack Ozcan did you?

ZABI. I am afraid he might be dead.
    I am afraid he might be dead.

    ZABI *puts his head into his hands.*

    The SHADOW BOY *comes to comfort him.*

Beat Eighteen

Past.

HANNAH *arrives to the bog where* HERR IRELAND *is footing turf. She has brought the shirt.*

HANNAH. Séan!

    HERR IRELAND *turns away.*

    Séan?

HERR IRELAND. I'm busy.
    (*In German.*) Can't you see I'm busy with work?

HANNAH (*in Irish*). Sorry… (*In English.*) but /

HERR IRELAND. Can't you see that I am working?
  I have to stack the turf while the weather is dry.

HANNAH. But… I want to say that I am sorry.
  So sorry about Peter.
  It is not like him. He is a good man.

HERR IRELAND. A good man?!

HANNAH. He is just concerned, concerned about these
  Houghers.

HERR IRELAND. Houghers?

HANNAH. Villains who attack our farms.

HERR IRELAND. O villains, is it?

HANNAH. They cut the legs of cattle.
  (*In Irish.*) They cut…

HERR IRELAND. And why do you think they do that, Hannah?

HANNAH. I don't know?! It is wanton! It is some strange evil
  or envy to hurt an animal, to destroy a livelihood.

HERR IRELAND. But what if the animal is devouring all of
  a man's pasture, Hannah? And what if the livelihood of your
  master or your husband means that the same man has to shift
  himself time and time again off good land. Time and time
  again up the hills where nothing grows. What then would
  you expect that man to do? Tip his cap? Bend and bless the
  master and his cattle and keep moving west in his hunger and
  submission till he falls off the earth altogether or back into
  the sea itself?

HANNAH. Why are you so angry?

HERR IRELAND. Your husband swung a bloody axe at me!

HANNAH. I don't understand you.

HERR IRELAND. No you don't.
  You don't understand and you never will.

HANNAH. Peter is a good man…

HERR IRELAND. So go home to him!
Go on the fuck home and don't be bothering me.

HANNAH. O my God! You! You are a Hougher?

HERR IRELAND. I am a Hougher?
Well now there's a thought. Am I a Hougher?
Do I understand their anger?
Do I understand their hunger?
Of course I do, but I also understand that when they're
caught they will be strung up without mercy! They will
be whipped and tortured by good men like your husband.
They'll be murdered in their dozens and then their severed
heads will be stuck up on a post as a warning to everyone
else. Because for every cow that is maimed, Hannah, your
master will butcher ten of us. Mark my words! Because your
master, YOUR Lord Southwell values the Irish less than
his cattle and any sign of resistance just gives him another
excuse to kill.

HANNAH. My Lord Southwell? He is not my Lord Southwell.

HERR IRELAND. He brought you here, didn't he?

HANNAH. Hate.
All I see in you now is hate.

HERR IRELAND. So go home.
Go home for God's sake.
You shouldn't be here.

HANNAH. But I thought we were friends.

HERR IRELAND. Is that really what we are?
Or am I something more to you?

She stands still looking at him.

She is obviously torn.

He puts out his hand to her but she cannot take it.

He shakes his head.

I cannot play these games, Hannah.

I have had my heart broken and it's taken me nearly thirty
years…
My heart won't take another /

HANNAH (*in Irish*). Heart?

HERR IRELAND. O, for God's sake. Stop!
Stop this nonsense and go home.
Go home to your good man and your empty life and leave
me be.
Leave me to my own people.

He turns away from her.

HANNAH *shudders. She is deeply wounded.*

*She places the shirt on a stone by the turf, turns and walks
away.*

Beat Nineteen

Present.

HANNAH *leaves the scene and returns to the present.*

She sees the SHADOW BOY *for the first time, hovering near*
ZABI.

HANNAH. Zabi?

MOLLY (*looking at her phone*). There are no reports of any
murders in Dublin.
I can find nothing about the attack.
Your friend must have got away, Zabi…

HANNAH. But who is this with you?

MOLLY. Ozcan must have got away too.

HANNAH. Who are you?

She shrieks.

Ludwig?

The SHADOW BOY *now spins away.*

MOLLY. Ludwig?

HANNAH. Ludwig? Is that you?
  Are you here?

  HANNAH *runs into the shed after the shadow.*

  MOLLY *and* ZABI *watch her return… frantic.*

  She turns to them.

  Ludwig's face is the face I cannot see.
  Why is this?
  When Ludwig's face is the face that I love most of all.
  Ludwig – with his young arms brown from the summer sun.
  Brown legs that grow in strength.
  Fast. The fastest to run. The fastest to plough.
  Ludwig – who can climb a haystack quicker than all the
  other boys.

MOLLY. Hannah…

HANNAH. Ludwig! – whose voice suddenly breaks into that of
  a man.
  His voice. I call it. I call it again and again. I beg it to travel
  back to me over the years but all I am met with are the
  whispers – whispers whispers whispers of the trees.
  Ludwig – his eyes are my eyes – my eyes looking back at me
  with love when he was little, with increasing confusion and
  defiance as he grows, and then with anger, such anger, such
  disgust when last I saw him.

MOLLY. Why do you torment yourself?

HANNAH. When I tried to stop him, Molly. When I struck him
  for the first time in my life. When I cursed at him, cursed and
  cursed into my own eyes, my own soul.

MOLLY. Shhhh… shhhh.

ZABI. What happened to Ludwig?

HANNAH. Houghers!

MOLLY. Houghers.

HANNAH. Houghers, Houghers, Houghers.

Beat Twenty

Present.

H IRELAND. Houghers! Young men fed up with the English
and their evictions, their high rents and brutal laws. My
cousins, my brothers, my neighbours. And I am afraid –
afraid for them. I warn them that the English will show no
mercy. Their actions will stir nothing but killing. But they
do not hear me. Emboldened by tales of success around
the country. Tales of rents reduced. Emboldened by the
moonlight. Emboldened by the permanent hunger that gnaws
away at all Irish happiness. Irish pride.

Beat Twenty-One

Past/present.

PETER *walks into* HANNAH*'s kitchen in a red yeomanry coat.*

HANNAH. What is this?

PETER. Ha! Do you like it?

HANNAH. Like it? It is a soldier's uniform?!

PETER. Yes.
    Lord Southwell has ordered them down from Dublin.
    We are to form a German militia to stop these Houghers!
    All members will wear them when out on parade!

HANNAH. Militia?!
    Parade? What is this, Peter?
    Why would you go out on parade?

PETER. To frighten the Irish. To frighten the Houghers,
    Hannah, and let them know that we are serious when it
    comes to protecting our farms.

HANNAH. A soldier's uniform, Peter! A soldier's uniform, like
the soldiers who stole from us, who murdered us back home!

PETER. This is different, Hannah. We have to protect ourselves.
Protect Lord Southwell because his land is our land now.
His safety is ours.

He exits.

HANNAH. No, no.
Peter!

HANNAH *follows him.*

Present.

ZABI. Soldier is a bad thing. I know soldier sometime can
be good but in my life a soldier is a bad thing. A soldier is
death. A soldier is war. I hide from soldiers in Pakistan, in
Turkey, in Bulgaria, in Serbia, in Austria, in Italy, in France.
I hide from soldier at borders, in the streets, in the camps.

HANNAH. I didn't marry a soldier.

MOLLY. Hannah didn't marry a soldier.

HANNAH. And I didn't come to Ireland to conquer or to steal
another family's future.

MOLLY. Or fall in another man's war.

HANNAH. I came here for refuge.

ZABI. Refuge.

MOLLY. Refuge.

HANNAH. So when I look into the scarlet shout of that coat in
my kitchen, I know it can only bring ruin.

The SHADOW BOY *flickers by again.*

Beat Twenty-Two

Present.

HERR IRELAND (*in Irish*). Parade.

MOLLY. Parade.

ZABI (*in Pashto*). Parade.

HERR IRELAND. Whistles and drums and coats and muskets.

HANNAH. Beware of the Papists. Beware of the Houghers.
    Beware of the Irish. They have blood on their hands!

HERR IRELAND. We have blood on our hands.

HANNAH. Massacre.

HERR IRELAND (*in Irish*). Massacre.

ZABI (*in Pashto*). Massacre.

HANNAH (*in German*). Massacre. A new word. An old word.
    A brutal word.

HERR IRELAND (*in Irish*). Massacre.

HANNAH. It becomes all the talk in our village. All the talk in
    the market, all the talk in our church, our gardens, our fields.
    The massacre of poor Protestants in Ireland by men like you.

HERR IRELAND. Men like me?

HANNAH (*in German*). Rebellion?

ZABI (*in Pashto*). Rebellion.

HERR IRELAND. Rebellion.
    It becomes all the talk in our village. All the talk in the
    taverns, the cottages, the mountains, the fields.
    Revenge for the persecution of our people.
    Revenge for the theft of our land.
    Eviction. Subjugation.

HANNAH. Ludwig comes home with stories of the drowning
    of poor Protestants. Of pregnant women ripped open by
    Houghers. Of cannibalism! Of babies hurled against rocks!

HERR IRELAND. English tales.

English lies living and breathing, made for mayhem and massacre.

HANNAH (*in Irish*). Massacre.

ZABI (*in Pashto*). Massacre.

HERR IRELAND. How? When all we have is a few desperate youths with blackened faces burning crops and not a gun between them!
Anger and courage are the Hougher's only weapon.

HANNAH. So it is anger and courage and lies that make for massacre.

ZABI. When I was a young boy, I had no school from the Taliban but learning the Koran. I had no school but learning how to be a soldier. How to be cleaning, holding, shooting a gun. I had no school but am told that my country is great, my country is 'the graveyard of empires', my country is the land of unbeatable warlords. All war it starts with stories, all war it starts with lies.

HANNAH. Stories of Hougher attacks grow in our village. Stories of Hougher attacks strike the quiet landscape like lightning, frightening us and fusing us more and more to Southwell's cause. I no longer walk along the river or up through the bogland. I no longer speak with Séan or the Irish. I no longer watch them sail between their small cabins of mud and thatch. And I no longer seek out their music as it swings stubbornly on the winds. I bury myself, like the good planter, in my work, in our community and in our church. But unlike my neighbours I can find no solace in it.

And now…

MOLLY. And now!

ZABI. And now?

HANNAH. Ludwig!

The SHADOW BOY *spins out of the barn again.*

Beat Twenty-Three

Past/present.

HERR IRELAND. I follow the Houghers over the fields.
I follow the Houghers in anger.
My heart, my head, blinded by revenge.

HANNAH (*in Irish*). Revenge.

MOLLY. Revenge.

HERR IRELAND. Like foxes – we move across the land.
Utter silence. Utter intent.

HANNAH. I hear something in the rafters.
Gentle at first.
Almost music. Almost a dance.
A rustle. A cackle.
Until it rises up…

HERR IRELAND. We know every ditch and every stream,
every rise and every trail. We don't even need moonlight to
show us the way because the bogs and stone and grasses are
sewn into our hearts, as familiar, even in darkness, as our
own breath, our own pulse, our own soul.

HANNAH. A rustle. A cackle. A dance… that rises up in
a devouring of wooden beams, wooden carts, wooden walls.
FIRE!
FIRE!

HERR IRELAND (*in Irish*). Fire.

HANNAH. Rising up like an inferno!

HERR IRELAND. Burn them out!

PETER. Hannah! Hannah!
Get up. Get up.
Quick, Ludwig. Come. Come with your mother.
Fire! Houghers! There is an attack.

HANNAH. We run out into the courtyard.
And see that it is the Leagers' barn that leaps in flame. Hans
Leager, his wife and daughters are running with buckets,

trying to quench the screaming blaze. Then gunshot. The shout of gunshot, the snort of horses as some of Southwell's militia come careering up the lane.

HERR IRELAND. I see that some of the boys have laid havoc on the cattle in the Palatine commonage. I see that they have set light to the Palatine barns but now they are caught in the circle of the village, their white smocks exposing them in the light of the fire.

PETER. Shoot! Shoot!

HERR IRELAND. Blood and bellowing.
Stampede.

HANNAH. Peter and the men run into formation with their coats and guns.
Peter and the men start to fire their muskets.

HERR IRELAND. All is mayhem.

PETER. As these Houghers run at us like malignant ghosts.
Run at us with sticks and scythes.

HERR IRELAND. They are trying to find a route out.

HANNAH. I am knocked to the ground as two of them fly over our small stone wall and away through the commonage to the fields.

HERR IRELAND. Hannah!

PETER. Chase! Give chase!

HANNAH. Peter, Alfred, Hans, all the men of the village, all running, all shooting.

HERR IRELAND. I see Hannah knocked to the ground.
Hannah! No!
What am I doing?

HANNAH. And Ludwig!

HERR IRELAND. The son.
The boy. Hannah's boy!

PETER. Chase! Give chase!

HERR IRELAND. Running toward me!

HANNAH. I pick myself up and catch him, catch Ludwig as he
tries to hurtle by with the other boys.

HERR IRELAND. All is carnage. All is flying fist and boot and
musket.

HANNAH. *No! No! You cannot go. Leave it to your father.
Leave it to the men.*
He tries to throw me off, Ludwig tries to throw me off but
I find strength I never knew. I tear at him, tear at my own
boy in an effort to save him, to keep him from harm.
But his eyes are furious. His eyes are wild.

'Get off me. Get off me, Mama.
You bring me nothing but shame.'

And he is gone.

PETER. Chase the Houghers!
Chase the Papists!

HERR IRELAND. We are forced to flee…

HANNAH. I am forced onto the village square with all the
other women. The air is thick with smoke. The horses charge
off through the fields, riders raging, riders shooting.

HERR IRELAND. Forced to flee toward the river.

HANNAH. The night becomes one great shout of unfamiliar
sound – unfamiliar voices, hooves, curses, flames – the little
ones are terrified – their mothers hold them, bury them deep
into their bodies – but where is mine?!

HERR IRELAND. I see more than one of our young Houghers
fall to blaring gunshot as we run. I lift a bleeding brother
onto my shoulder.
Then I see him.
I see Hannah's boy on the banks of the river with a musket in
his hand.
He seems to have lost his companions.
He points the gun toward us but he doesn't know how to fire.

In a moment our men are on him.
In a moment they have forced him to the ground.
All is young limbs and violent scream.
I run toward them, but I am too slow with the weight that is
on me. I try to shout a warning, I try…

There is the sound of a shot.

Then it stops. They stop.
They fall asunder in the shock of a shot.
And there is blood. A flow of blood now snaking from them.
The two Houghers, my cousins, stand.
Hannah's boy remains lifeless on the ground.

*A low keening rises up – a song or music filled with
mourning overwhelms the action, overwhelms the
auditorium, lasting quite some time.*

Beat Twenty-Four

Present.

HANNAH. It is Séan who takes me to find Ludwig.

HERR IRELAND. Peter and the militia are up at the castle.

PETER. Handing over our captives like an offering to
    Southwell.

HANNAH. My Ludwig.

PETER. I'm sorry, Hannah.

HANNAH. Bloody and broken.

HERR IRELAND. I'm so sorry.

HANNAH. My Ludwig.

PETER. Please forgive me.

HANNAH. Pale as the morning.

PETER/HERR IRELAND. I didn't know that he would follow.

HANNAH. My Ludwig.
Motionless.
All life, all his life, my life,
now drained away into this Irish soil.

ZABI *approaches* HANNAH.

ZABI. You come to Ireland because you love your son.
All you do is because you love your son.
You pack his things.
You buy him shoes.
You say,
'It is cold over there, you must wear these shoes.'
He still feels your love.
He still knows your love.

HANNAH. No, I failed him.
I failed both my sons.

Beat Twenty-Five

Past.

We are back in Hannah's kitchen, it is after Ludwig's death.

PETER. Hannah.

She sits in her chair, silent, unresponsive.

Hannah. Pastor Geyer says he will come again tonight to
pray with us.
Pastor Geyer… /

HANNAH. I have told you that I do not want to see him.
I have told you that I do not want to see any of them.

PETER. They are family. They are neighbours.

HANNAH. I have no family, Peter.
All is lost.

Lost to the ground and lost to the gun.
Your gun.

PETER (*shaking his head*). Please.

HANNAH. Your musket.
Your pride and your ambition.
That is what brought killing into this house.

PETER. Hannah, please… /

HANNAH. Hannah please!
Hannah please!
Hannah lie with me.
Hannah give me a child.
Hannah give me your heart. Give me your life!
You took everything, Peter. Take everything.
You and your God!

PETER. You cannot say that.
God is the truth and the light.
God is /

HANNAH. A merciless killer.
God is a taker of children.
I have no interest in your God.

PETER (*in increasing panic*). Please, please. Whatever about
me, you cannot turn against God, Hannah. You cannot deny
him.

HANNAH. But I do, Peter.
I do deny him.
I spit in his face!

PETER *strikes* HANNAH *across the face in his shock at her
words.*

Then instantly regrets it.

PETER. No. No. I'm sorry. O no, how could I do such a thing.
I shouldn't, I never… I can never hurt you.

HANNAH *stands in silence looking straight at him.*

Then turns to exit.

Hannah! No! Hannah. Where are you going?
You cannot leave the house.
It is almost night.

She is gone.

Hannah, don't you think I miss him too?
Don't you think that I grieve them both too?
Ludwig.
Albert.

He puts his hands to his head.

My son. My sons.
All I do! All of this!
It is nothing. It is nothing, without you.

Present.

HERR IRELAND. Hannah marches out from her Palatine
house.
Hannah marches tall into the evening light.
Hannah marches with all the strength that is left to her in her
long strides.

PETER. Long strides.

HANNAH. To the river.

MOLLY. To the river.
To the place where her little *Catach* had fallen.

HERR IRELAND. Here.

PETER. Here.

Beat Twenty-Six

Present.

HERR IRELAND. Once again, I am too late.

PETER. Too late.

HERR IRELAND. Too late to stop you.

PETER (*in German*). Too late to stop you

HERR IRELAND. Floating skirts and floating hair dashed on
stone.
Bloody and broken, just like your son.
Pale as the morning, just like your son.

PETER. When I get to the river.
I see the Irish man.
I see him standing in the shallows with Hannah in his arms.
And I see his tears fall and bleed away into the same waters
that took her.

MOLLY. Side by side now they stand.

HERR IRELAND. Side by side.

MOLLY. The two men.
When all the killing is over.

ZABI *approaches* HANNAH.

ZABI. Over. It is over.
Why do you not go to him?
To Ludwig?

HANNAH. Because he is lost to me.

ZABI. But he is here!

MOLLY. He has always been here.

ZABI. 'Mama,' he says.
'Mama.'

PETER/ZABI (*together*). It is over.

PETER. It is time.
Come back to us.

HANNAH. But I cannot forgive.

ZABI. Yet he forgives?

HERR IRELAND. Listen to him.
Listen to the boy, Hannah.

(*In Irish.*) Listen.

> It is time.
> Time to let go of this place.
> To give yourself peace.
> Give us all peace.

MOLLY. Peace, Hannah.

HERR IRELAND. You have paid and repaid all debt to this
world.

MOLLY. You have saved this boy.
Another boy.

ZABI. You, I, please.
Let us take this gift of peace.
(*In Pashto.*) Peace.

The SHADOW BOY *approaches* HANNAH.

HANNAH. Ludwig?!

MOLLY. Take his hand, Hannah.

PETER. Please, my love.

HERR IRELAND. Please.

PETER. Take his hand.
And come back to us.

HANNAH *takes the hand of her son.*

MOLLY *takes the hand of* ZABI.

MOLLY. Will you come with me now?

ZABI. I will.

MOLLY. No more running.

ZABI. No more running.

HANNAH (*in Irish*). Peace.

ZABI (*in Pashto*). Peace.

MOLLY. Peace.

And so both pairs walk away into the skies and their future.

End.

A Nick Hern Book

Refuge first published in Great Britain as a paperback original in 2026 by Nick Hern Books Limited, The Glasshouse, 49a Goldhawk Road, London, in association with Fishamble: The New Theatre Company

Refuge copyright © 2026 Deirdre Kinahan

Deirdre Kinahan has asserted her right to be identified as the author of this work

Cover photograph: Andreas J. Etter
Illustration of Hannah von Peinen by Steve Wickham

Designed and typeset by Nick Hern Books, London
Printed in Great Britain by Mimeo Ltd, Huntingdon, Cambridgeshire PE29 6XX

A CIP catalogue record for this book is available from the British Library

ISBN 978 1 83904 589 9

www.nickhernbooks.co.uk/environmental-policy

Nick Hern Books' authorised representative in the EU is
Easy Access System Europe – Mustamäe tee 50, 10621 Tallinn, Estonia
email gpsr.requests@easproject.com